AF516320

THE ZEN WAY TO BE AN EFFECTIVE MANAGER

THE ZEN WAY TO BE AN EFFECTIVE MANAGER

Radha

Viva Books Private Limited
New Delhi • Mumbai • Chennai • Kolkata • Bangalore

Copyright © Mercury Books

First Indian Edition 1993

Reprinted 2004

VIVA BOOKS PRIVATE LIMITED

- 4262/3 Ansari Road, Daryaganj, New Delhi 110 002
  E-mail: viva@vivagroupindia.net
- 215-216 New Apollo Estate, 2nd Floor, Mogra Lane, Andheri (E), Mumbai 400 069
  E-mail: vivamumbai@vivagroupindia.net
- Jamal Fazal Chambers, 26 Greams Road, Chennai 600 0067
  E-mail: vivachennai@vivagroupindia.net
- B-103, Jindal Towers, 21/1A/3, Darga Road, Kolkata-700 017
  E-mail: vivakolkata@vivagroupindia.net
- 7 GF, Sovereign Park Apts., 56-58 K. R. Road, Basavanagudi, Bangalore 560 004
  Email: vivabangalore@vivagroupindia.net

Published by arrangement with

Mercury Books
Gold Arrow Publications Limited
862 Garratt Lane, London SW17 0NB

All rights reserved. No part of this publication may be reproduced, stored in a retrieval system, or transmitted in any form or by any means, electronic, mechanical, photocopying, recording, or otherwise without the prior permission of the publishers.

This book is sold subject to the condition that it shall not, by way of trade or otherwise, be lent, re-sold, hired out or otherwise circulated without the publisher's prior consent in any form of binding or cover other than that in which it is published and without a similar condition including this condition being imposed upon the subsequent purchaser.

This edition is licensed for sale in India, Pakistan, Bangladesh, Sri Lanka and Nepal only.
Not for export elsewhere.

ISBN 81-7649-649-9

Published by Vinod Vasishtha for Viva Books Private Limited, 4262/3 Ansari Road, New Delhi 110 002 and printed at Rajkamal Electric Press, Delhi 1100 33.

Today's world is filled with knowledge. Knowledge and wisdom, I think, have to be considered on different levels. In our highly developed world, knowledge can usually be easily obtained if one so desires and makes the effort. It is wisdom, however, that enables one to apply acquired knowledge and give it value. Knowledge is obtained by reading books and newspapers, watching television, hearing lectures, and so on. But knowledge in itself is empty. To be of value it must be put into practice and continuously applied in response to ever-changing circumstances. This, then, is wisdom. It is the best application of knowledge.

Soshitsu Sen

The illustrations in this book
are by Christine Braig.

Contents

Introduction

The Way is as Clear as Daylight

Any basic truth may be considered as an obvious platitude or a profound way of life. Zen is a perfect example of this, for it is so blindingly obvious that we have a hard time believing it. The message of Zen is, 'Be simple, don't be hung up on particular thoughts and sensations. Do not be a slave to your own responses – they come and go simply as reflections of circumstances. Just be natural and spontaneous in everything you do.' It sounds easy – until you try. For when you try to be natural, you are not! Zen shows us the way out of this dilemma. And that is what this book is about.

But unfortunately the word 'Zen', like the Chinese word 'Tao', has come to be employed as a fashionable advertising slogan, for everything Japanese is 'in'. Even in Japan itself this has happened. One well-known cosmetics firm markets a perfume as 'Zen – a great new classic fragrance', and in many European countries watches are advertised as 'telling the eternal Tao'. (Warning: the first line of the great Chinese classic work called *Tao Te Ching* tells us the 'The Tao which can be told is not the eternal Tao'!) Yet the teaching of Zen is one of the great spiritual traditions of the world, and so if I am to be cleared of the accusation of misusing the word merely to help in the marketing of yet another book on management, I must state my position quite openly. Or rather, I must show justification from within the Zen tradition itself, and here I can base myself on the great Zen scholar Daisetz T. Suzuki:

> The characteristic difference between Zen and all other teachings of a religious or philosophical kind is that it never vanishes from our daily life, and yet amongst all the practical possibilities of its application and with all its concreteness, it contains something which can emerge from the spectacle of world defilement and restlessness.[1]

Zen, then, is a quality of life which is concrete and practical, and so the life and spirit of Zen is to be found in artists, poets, swordsmen and archers, carpenters, builders and merchants, as we shall see. It is precisely this presence of Zen in ordinary everyday life with which this book is concerned, for the entire tradition of Zen stresses that it is 'nothing special, it is just everyday mind'. And so, just as Miyamoto Musashi instructed swordsmen in his *Book of Five Rings* and the monk Soshan Suzuki gave advice to merchants, this book is addressed to managers.

If we ask now what is the 'something special which can emerge . . . from nothing special', we can say that it is clarity displacing confusion, and the finding of a natural rhythm of alternation between stillness and purposeful activity. These are potential qualities which exist in all of us, but because we are frequently alienated from them, Zen proposes how we should realise them. We will then be able to use to the full, not only our powers of reasoning, but also those of intuition and creativity. In this way we become truly human.

Inner peace within the surrounding chaos

Most managers overlook the fact that they have only one person to lead – themselves. This was pointed out by Peter Drucker, one of the greatest of all management consultants, whose books, though written more than twenty-five years ago, are still standard texts. That managers do not realise this is hardly surprising, for time is not on their side. The rate of change in all the fields which affect management, technology, information processing and transmission, in the economic, social, political and environmental fields, is now so great that it is a superhuman task to keep up with it, even in one's own field. The days are long gone when it was necessary to keep pointing out that we live in a world of change; the question today is one of how we can maintain an even keel amongst the cross currents of change. But the manager has very little time, if any, to reflect on this, and instead tends to grab hold of any technique of thinking which seems to offer some degree of security – above all if it is new. What actually happens is that many turn not to one but to a succession of modish techniques – the resulting confusion is then worse than ever.

Zen changes this situation by maintaining inner peace within the surrounding chaos, and this enables the manager to use all his or her knowledge, training, experience and faculties more freely and effectively than ever before. It frees the manager from old, outdated habits of thought which we all inevitably acquire, and this allows him or her to perceive and assess every situation clearly and without distortion by preconceived ideas, and then *act* exactly in accord with it. There is, however, more to be said than this, for if Zen was only a method of obtaining tranquillity, it could not be distinguished from many other traditions, not to speak of the many techniques of meditation and relaxation which are used for this purpose. Zen asks us to become fully aware of the processes of our mind, not theoretically, but in actual practice. And even beyond that, to experience, learn and accept the limitations of that most highly regarded of all our faculties – reason. That reason does indeed have its limitations has been noted by many thinkers, among them Blaise Pascal, who said: 'The final step that reason can take is the recognition that there is an innumerable host of things which are beyond its reach.' That is not to say that such things are beyond our comprehension as human beings, but rather that rationality has its limitations. But this definitely does not mean that Zen is *ir*rational, and it is important to point this out, because most managers either look down on or actually fear the irrational, which they regard as something they cannot control. For after all, their training is entirely directed towards the use of reasoning power to control their environment, so that anything which is an apparent threat to this will be resisted. But rationality cannot in fact give us a complete and accurate picture of the real world for two reasons. Firstly, the number of facts required for such a description is infinitely large, as Pascal said, and we have no way of telling whether *our particular selection* is the best possible (the impossibility of 100 per cent accurate weather forecasting is an example of this). Secondly, many of the elements of which the real world is composed are not susceptible to reason – elements such as emotions, feelings and preferences have an influence just as much as 'hard' facts, and these are not *ir*rational but *non*-rational. Zen, therefore, is not irrational, but accepts the rational while at the same time recognising the non-rational, of which we must be fully aware if we are to be truly effective in what we do.

What is Zen?

If Zen is non-rational, then no reasoned answer to this question is possible; any reasoned attempt to explain it will fail. It is therefore entirely logical (!) that Zen Masters, in reply to this question, give answers such as 'the cypress tree in the yard', or respond by some apparently crazy piece of spontaneous behaviour such as putting their sandals on their heads. In this they are demonstrating that no spoken – that is, rational – answer is possible, and that one can only know Zen by actual experiencing. Such experiencing must, however, go beyond what we regard as normal – it is the difference between seeing distant mountains on an averagely clear day and on one when one feels one could actually touch them.

There are many ways to this experiencing. That which is indicated, that is *pointed to*, in this book, is based on the principle of all Zen training, which is knowing, shaping and freeing the mind. (You may like to reflect on this in the light of recent developments in chaos theory.) We begin with knowing, but this is not enough. We may write and read books about Zen and the mind, but just as we may talk about water and describe it intelligently, this is not the same as swimming in it. To know what is, means experiencing it in its actual concreteness. No cookery book satisfies our hunger – only real food will do that.

Your commitment and what you may gain

If you have read stories of how Zen monks suddenly experienced 'enlightenment' on hearing a frog jump into a pool, seeing a falling leaf or even having their noses twisted by the master, now is the time to forget them. For what is usually not related in these anecdotes is just how long and hard the 'enlightened' one had to work before the sudden change took place. Anyone who believes that he or she can be 'transformed' without such work will inevitably be disappointed, and a great deal of work is therefore suggested in this book. What will it bring you?

I make no pretence that this book offers anyone the hope of 'enlightenment' or 'satori', as it is called in Zen, though I believe that those who wish eventually to go further in what is, after, all a spiritual practice will at least have started off in the right direction.[2] On the other hand, there is a great deal to be gained from *doing the work of training itself*, provided that you commit yourself to it, persist and carry your effort through. Zen in itself is not work, but it demands a determined commitment. The benefits to be obtained are effectiveness, clarity and sincerity, as well as an improved ability to withstand stress and to live with the uncertainties of daily life. To get a preliminary idea of what this can mean, ask yourself this question: What is the difference between a manager who is effective and one who is merely efficient?

The culture of the mind

It may seem surprising that the word 'meditation', except for a passing reference, does not appear in this book – of all things, in a book about Zen! There are good reasons for this. 'Meditation' is a Western word, and not a very good equivalent of what is meant in Buddhism as a whole or in Zen in particular, for it has come to be associated with a whole host of techniques of *escaping from daily life*, whether in a temple or a far-off cave in the Himalayas, or by escape into a state of trance or ecstasy; the term is also used for relaxation techniques, which it is surely better to speak of as such. In Pali, the language of the earliest (still current) Buddhist texts, *bhavana* is used, which means the culture or development of the mind. This expresses the purpose of this book and also its method, for the culture of the mind, that is to say, the process of making it a more fruitful 'field' for all our activities, is surely of the highest value to managers. It is not enough to learn management techniques – they must also have the right conditions to grow and to flourish.

Zen training

There are various ways of training. There is that of the monk who sits doing nothing more than experiencing his breathing, often for years. There is the way of the *koan*, in which the monk spends a great deal of time trying to answer questions to which there is no logical answer, such as the well-known one, 'what is the sound of one hand clapping?', until he realises *out of his own experience*, that no answer is possible; this can be a sudden breakthrough into clarity. And then there are ways of action, through martial arts such as archery and swordfighting, and more peaceful ones, such as painting, calligraphy and pottery.

But very few managers have time to sit doing nothing or to struggle with unanswerable questions, nor do they wish to devote themselves to the arts. Therefore our way is through simple ordinary living and working as a manager. For those who might regard this as not 'Zen', remembering after all the numerous books on 'Zen in the art of...', let me assure them that the Way of the Manager is well recognised in Zen tradition, as we shall see. And the role of the book is no more than that of a signpost: follow the direction indicated, but test every step of the way in the light of your experience in daily living, for the essential point of Zen is finding out for yourself.

Advice from the masters

The samurai (warrior) Miyamoto Musashi wrote in his *Book of Five Rings*:

> Language does not extend to explaining the Way in detail but it can be grasped intuitively. Study this book; read a word then ponder on it . . . Absorb the things written in this book. Do not just read, memorise or imitate, but so that you realise the principle from within your own heart, study hard to absorb these things into your body.[3]

There is a particular attitude I would ask you to avoid in reading this book. Do not think of yourself as a manager trying to 'get Zen' and developing effectiveness. You are a whole person who plays many roles, and effectiveness is an affair of the whole person. You cannot put it on with your business suit and tie – and if you try to do that, there is no Zen. But the point was far better made by an old Zen Master:

A high official once visited Master Keichu. He waited while his card was taken in to the Master, who looked at it. It said, 'Kitagaki, Governor of Kyoto'. 'Who is that person?' said the Master, 'he has no business here, send him away.' The attendant took the card back to the Master, who, seeing his mistake, scratched out the words 'Governor of Kyoto', and the card was once more taken in to the Master, who said, 'Ah yes, I want to see that fellow. Show him in.'

Zen – the letter and the spirit

The word Zen can be used in various ways. It may refer to the teaching of Zen, to the various schools and traditions and to the culture of Zen. Here, we are using it to indicate a quality of mind and spirit. From much that is written and said of Zen, one would suppose that it is something exclusively Japanese and Chinese. This is certainly true of its schools, traditions and culture and of course of the primary literature of Zen. But when we look at it more deeply we find that the spirit of Zen is *universal*, for because it is not merely a teaching but a quality of human nature it is not restricted to any one race, culture or period of history. It just so happens that Zen found its clearest and most comprehensive expression in the east, but one can also find the spirit of Zen in western literature. One might for example mention the American writer Thoreau here, and of course there is much in the Bible which has the same meaning, if not the same flavour.

Zen originated from the encounter of Buddhism, brought by monks from India to China, with Taoism and Chinese outlook and culture in general. Therefore the sources of inspiration and the quotations in this book are not restricted to the 'Zen tradition' as generally recognised (that is to say, Japanese). Much comes from early Buddhist and Taoist writings, all of which are living aspects of Zen. The aim is to find expressions of the spirit of Zen *which would be understandable to managers in our Western world.* This is the real point – it has been said that 'Zen is as close to you as breathing'. Why then, allow any barriers to comprehension such as cultural differences and ways of thinking which do not happen to be our own to stand in the way? Alternatively, nothing is to be gained by adapting or imitating the outward signs of Zen. You cannot get Zen' by sleeping on a futon bed surrounded by Japanese lanterns!

In a famous quotation, Zen is said to be a 'special transmission without scriptures', meaning that ultimately it moves only 'from heart to heart', and so its final transmission can only be non-verbal. But this need not surprise even the most hard-bitten 'realist', for we are well accustomed to the idea that 'body-language', for example a smile, can communicate things which cannot be expressed in words (see chapter 'Zen des Lachens' in the author's book *Aufs Herz vertrauen* ['Trust in the Heart'], Hermann Bauer Verlag, Freiburg). Yet much can be expressed through art, and so a painting has been placed at the beginning of each chapter to try to make good the failings of words. Each was painted specially by a western artist who has chosen to express herself in the spirit of the early Chinese Zen painters, without slavishly copying their manner or their subjects. Perhaps this is the opportunity to express my deep appreciation of the way in which she spent many, many hours repeating each painting until 'the right one' appeared under her brush.

PART 1 – ZEN IS . . .

The Zen painter can capture a graceful bamboo with a few swift strokes of his brush.

The manager who 'has Zen' sees everything clearly and catches the essence of a situation.

He can define it like the artist.

Chapter 1

The Way of Effectiveness

Effectiveness reveals itself as crucial to a man's self-development; to organisation development and to the fulfilment and viability of modern society.

Peter Drucker[1]

If one is a true follower of the Way one does not search for the faults of the world, but speedily applies oneself to attaining genuine insight. If one can see with perfect clarity, then all is completed.

Rinzai Gigen[2]

The whole essence of this book is contained in these two quotations. Yet their authors are very different. Peter Drucker and his work had a profound influence on management, on industry as a whole and therefore ultimately on society.[3] For, as Drucker continued, 'As executives work towards becoming effective, they raise the performance level of the whole organisation. They raise the sights of people – of others as well as their own.' Rinzai, in contrast, was a Chinese monk, a Zen Master who lived in the ninth century and founded one of the

'Five Houses of Zen', the Rinzai Line. Some 300 years later this school of Zen was brought to Japan; it still flourishes there and also has followers in the west.

Seen in this way, Zen is – or it is better to say, results in – nothing more or less than *genuine insight*, and this is the key to *effectiveness*. Without this a manager, however technically competent he is and however much authority he has, is of no value to his organisation – or indeed to himself. The days are long past when the art of management was to find the most profitable ways of getting others to do the work. Today the manager lives in a world of ever-increasing scientific, technological and sociological complexity, which, through its enormously dynamic expansion, is in danger of destroying itself. And so the challenge to the manager is to utilise every faculty of his or her being so as to be able to perceive the situation both in its widest aspects and its smallest details, and then to *act*. It is not enough to develop and acquire new management techniques, important and essential as they may be, for without the quality of *effectiveness* in those who use them they are, to use the expression of an old Zen Master, 'dead words'.

But then we ask, what actually is effectiveness? It is not something which can be defined and measured; directly we attempt to do so we find we are measuring something quite different – *efficiency*. Efficiency is certainly part of effectiveness, but there is much more. This, even if we cannot define it, we can certainly see in action, and nowhere better than in the Zen arts of China and Japan. There is the swordfighter, whose weapon swings 'as though it had a soul of its own' (Suzuki), so that all the experience and skill he has acquired during his training acts through his intuitive, instant perception of the situation. The Zen painter can capture a leaping cat or a graceful bamboo with a few swift strokes of his brush on the paper, and the music of the flute-player floats weightlessly through the air. And so the effective manager uses his whole knowledge, experience and power of thought like the sword or the brush. He sees everything clearly and catches the essence of a situation, and can define it like the artist. And he communicates like the flute.

The secret of nourishing life

Less warlike than the sword is the butcher's knife, and a delightful description comes to us from the early Chinese Taoist philosopher Chuang Tzu:

> Cook Ting was cutting up an ox for Lord Wen-Hui. At every touch of his hand, every heave of his shoulder, every move of his feet, every thrust of his knee – zip! zoop! He slithered the knife along with a zing and all was in perfect rhythm, as though he were performing the dance of the Mulberry Grove or keeping time to the ching-shou music.
>
> 'Ah, this is marvellous,' said Lord Wen-Hui, 'imagine skill reaching such heights!'
>
> Cook Ting laid down his knife and replied, 'What I care about is the Way which goes beyond skill. When I first began cutting up oxen, all I could see was the ox itself. After three years I no longer saw the whole ox. And now – I go at it with spirit and don't look with my eyes. Perception and understanding have come to a stop and spirit moves where it wants. I go along with the natural make-up, strike in the big hollows, guide the knife through the big openings, and follow things as they are. So I never touch the smallest ligament or tendon, much less a main joint.
>
> 'A good cook changes his knife once a year – because he cuts. A mediocre cook changes his knife once a month – because he hacks. I've had this knife of mine for nineteen years and I've cut up thousands of oxen with it, and yet the blade is as good as though it had just come from the grindstone. There are spaces between the joints, and the blade of the knife really has no thickness. If you insert what has no thickness into such spaces, then there's plenty of room – more than enough for the blade to play about it. That's why

after nineteen years the blade of my knife is still as good as when it came from the grindstone.

'However, whenever I come to a complicated place, I size up the difficulties, tell myself to watch out and be careful, keep my eyes on what I'm doing, work very slowly, and move the knife with the greatest subtlety until - flop! the whole thing comes to the ground . . . and then I wipe off the knife and put it away.'

'Excellent!', said Lord Wen-Hui. 'I have heard the words of Cook Ting and learned the secret of nourishing life.'[4]

The real question for us here is, why are we not as effective as Cook Ting? Why are we 'mediocre cooks' whose knives get blunt, or just 'good cooks' for whom the only way is to keep finding new recipes?

Exercise: At various points in this book you will be asked to do exercises. They consist in stopping reading and considering what has just gone before. It is worth spending some time on this, even laying the book aside for a day or two while you simply bear the questions in mind, and think about them during an odd moment. If you find it useful to jot down a few notes, this is a good idea. Be sure to include the date of writing, and review your notes later on. To begin. What does Cook Ting mean when he says that 'perception and understanding have come to a stop'? When he mentions the blade of his knife, he says it *has no thickness*, and not that it is very thin. What is the difference? And the main question – are you a mediocre manager, or a good one – or do you work like Cook Ting?

The story of Cook Ting exactly illustrates the meaning of the Chinese expression *wu-wei*. *Wu* means 'not' and *wei* means 'action, making, doing, striving, straining or busyness'. A good example would be when we try to see a distant object, such as a noticeboard. If we strain to see it, the eyes very quickly become tired and we cannot read it; instead, the eyes must be relaxed, so that we are not staring, not *making any effort*. Equally, this applies to peripheral vision, which is the ability to see things which are not in the direct line of sight on which we are concentrating. It is really this which Cook Ting means by 'not looking with his eyes', without, of course, meaning that his eyes are closed. He is not straining to see. He is aware of the whole ox, and is not simply concentrating only on the point where he is cutting, and in this way he is able to 'go along with the natural make-up'.

It is the ability to 'look without looking' that is one of the vital differences between the effective and the efficient manager. The latter concentrates so much on the task which he has clearly defined that he fails to see both the wider aspects which affect it or the global effects which his decision or plan will have. This is often a recipe for disaster, as for instance when an organisation plan for a department is worked out without awareness of the characters of the people who will have to fit into the plan, or without taking fully into account the effects on other departments.

What prevents us from being effective?

Lord Wen-Hui's final comment on Cook Ting may have struck you as a little odd. How can a butcher be said to be 'nourishing life'? Kuang-Ming Wu explains that not only did the cook feed Lord Wen-hui with the *result* of his act (food for physical life), but also fed him with the *words* of his act (food for life-nourishment). And the act is that of the bloody undoing of an ox!

The life of which we are talking is *naturalness*, which is acting as we are – with all our skills and good qualities (and equally with our limitations and faults) – without forcing ourselves into any rigid mould of behaviour. And this is, equally, effectiveness. But however much we may admire Cook Ting, we cannot become effective by trying to be effective! We cannot plan to be natural. For, if I try to be natural, my trying is itself unnatural, and I am being affected. The same is true of sincerity; when someone says he will *try to be sincere* with you, you know very well that sincerity is the last thing you can expect!

This paradoxical and frustrating situation is due to an elementary mistake. The human mind has the ability to stand apart from itself, be aware of itself and criticise its own processes, that is to say, it has a 'feed-back'system. Like all such systems – a room-thermostat would be a simple example – the mind's feedback system must be set; settings must be made which establish the degree of naturalness, sincerity or effectiveness at any given moment. But now *another* feedback system is required, this time to set the settings, and another will be needed to correct the second, and so on *ad infinitum*. Such a series of control systems becomes frustrated by its own complexity; it is not possible to correct one's means of self-correction indefinitely. Therefore, when a manager thinks too minutely and in too great detail about a decision to be made, he or she will not be able to decide until *forced to do so by the pressure of time*. At that moment the manager acts naturally, for there is no other choice; the decision may not be the optimum one, for now he or she is not acting out of naturalness, but in panic. The manager is now the cook who hacks.

Exercise: This is not easy to understand on first reading. Think about it for a while and then see if you have experienced this process at work in yourself. Then ask, what is the final authority in the process of deciding? How far can you pass the buck, as Americans say? (President Truman had a sign on his desk that read: 'The buck stops here').

A feedback system can be rendered ineffective in another way. In order for it to function properly, there must be a margin of error. If, for example, the upper and lower limits on a thermostat are both set at 20°, the signal 'heating on' will coincide with 'heating off', and the system will rapidly alternate between 'on' and 'off' until it breaks down altogether. This situation resembles human anxiety, a state in which one is so self-conscious and makes such strong efforts to control oneself that there is a continual dithering between opposites. The manager who is trying to convince the boss that he or she deserves a higher salary may well fall victim to this, since at the crucial interview he or she is determined to show himself as perfectly self-controlled, but the effect may be quite the opposite of what is intended.

Let's go into that situation more deeply. What the aspirant to more pay has done is to construct, from past ideas, a mental image from his past ideas of exactly how he should behave. Quite possibly he has rehearsed the interview in his mind several times beforehand, and he tries to identify himself during the interview with the image of himself he has constructed, because he wants to present himself to the boss as 'effective'. Any deviation from that model at once creates loss of confidence and anxiety, and the whole effect is lost.

Exercise: What situations of this nature have you experienced? For instance, one might have happened during a meeting with an important customer; ask yourself, what are you actually selling? A product or service, certainly, but are you not also selling yourself? If you agree that this is so, then how do you go about it?

Being, but not becoming, effective

It must be obvious by now that there is no possible strategy for developing effectiveness, no way in which to create *wu-wei*. For any predetermined strategy at once brings our mental centre of gravity to the controller which controls what 'I' do, instead of allowing what 'I' am to act naturally. But acting naturally is precisely what we want. Let us try a little experiment:

Do something natural now!

It is of course quite impossible, for immediately you will begin to try to think of something natural to do; then it will not be natural at all. If I had asked you to do something spontaneous, or something unintentional, the result would have been the same. On the other hand, we are doing things naturally nearly all the time – you for example are turning the pages of this book quite naturally. What is the answer? In order to be natural, to be effective, to act like Cook Ting, there is no need to try, and as we now know, any effort to try prevents us from being natural. But as soon as we realise that willed and purposeful action happens 'by itself', that is, naturally, just as we breathe, see and feel naturally, we are no longer in the trap of trying to be natural. Zen does not seek to eliminate conscious and rational thought, but rather to allow the natural, intuitive powers to act through it. A simple example will make this clear: we all walk naturally, but use our reason to decide in which direction to go, how fast and so on.

It is impossible to become effective. You can only be it. And therefore the 'secret' of being an effective manager is to give up trying to be effective in the sense of modelling yourself on some concept of effectiveness, even that of Cook Ting. Just as he needed the skills of a butcher, so you require your managerial and other skills, but when you have them, you must forget that you have them, in the sense of just using them naturally and spontaneously, of allowing them to do their work. That is the 'blade which has no thickness'.

But if there is no *becoming* effective, there is nevertheless a Way of Effectiveness. Let us take our two 'thermostat' problems first. The answer to the first one is quite simply that ultimately there is nothing we can trust except ourselves, and it is no use trying to 'grasp the mind with the mind'. All you can do is, in the words of a Zen poem, is to 'sit quietly, doing nothing . . . spring comes and the grass grows by itself'. Which, as you now know, does *not* mean inactivity, but allowing the mind to 'happen'.

The second problem was that of over-sensitivity. Here, the answer is to be more flexible – or as it was previously said, to be more 'elastic'. Here this means to take a less fixed view of what you 'ought' to be, how you should behave, for example during that all-important interview. For, after all, however good your mental rehearsal was, however well you know your boss, there is always the element of the unpredictable. Your carefully worked out tactics and phrases simply may not fit the actual situation as it develops, but if you hold on to them tightly, determined that these *and no others* represent you (and your case for having a higher salary) you are doomed even before you start. Instead, you must be like a good lawyer, who has prepared his case well, so that when it comes to the actual day in court, he can 'think on his feet'.

And finally, to return to the 'sitting quietly, doing nothing'. What this really means is being able to discover all these tricks which the mind plays. How we can do this we will discover in the chapters on 'Sincerity' and 'Mindfulness'.

Exercise: Try to remember previous situations in which your mind actually has played the tricks described. You are looking for occasions on which things went badly wrong. How might they have gone better? But, please, do not occupy yourself with regrets, for the words, 'If only . . .' are the saddest – and also the most useless – in the English language! This will help you to be penetratingly honest with yourself, which is what is actually needed.

The object of Zen is to give space to all our creative impulses.

Chapter 2

The Way of Clarity

> What a difference, what a difference! I roll up the blind and I see the world. If anyone asks me what teaching it is I've grasped, I'll take my whisk and bash him in the mouth!
>
> *Zen Master Bankei*[1]

As will have been gathered from the introduction, this book is not about Zen, in the sense of giving its history, explaining its philosophy, describing its practices or presenting Zen literature, and the reader who wants to inform him or herself about these aspects had far better turn elsewhere – the choice is rich. Neither is the book about art, not even Zen art, though from this there comes much inspiration. And it is not intended to be yet another drop in the ocean of books about management; if the reader, whether in a small business or in a mighty corporation, is seeking new management techniques or even fresh business concepts, he or she will be disappointed. They will find more to their taste the latest issue of the *Harvard Business Review* which has just reached them after a suspiciously rapid transit across the desks of the Mighty Ones.

Essentially, this is a book about mind. It is particularly directed to the mind of the manager, but this is somewhat deceptive, for in reality there is no such thing as a manager-mind. The mind of the manager is the same as that of the 'ordinary' person; true, the manager has a certain stock of training and experience within his or her mind, but that is not at all the same thing; it cannot be identified with mind. Having said that we are discussing mind, it might be thought that the book is about psychology. But what is psychology about? Essentially, about *theories* of the structure and behaviour of mind, and there are as many different psychologies as there are theorists to construct them. Zen is neither a theory nor a structural concept. Zen is quality of mind, not a theory, but a fact. And although the teachings of Zen are many and varied, these are not what matters – as Bankei said.

Zen is quality of mind in the same sense that clarity is a quality of water or glass. But now, is it possible to define or measure clarity? You may surprise yourself with the answer – obviously, clarity cannot be defined, still less measured; it cannot even be described. But if we say that Zen is indescribable, we will at once get the reply that it must be something mystical or metaphysical, and certainly not something which managers need concern themselves with. Very well!

Question: What is the taste of a banana? Something very concrete and real. But can you describe it to me so that I can experience its taste? You can in fact only describe it in relative terms, such as 'sweeter than a lemon' and 'softer than an apple' and so on. In fact, if you want me to know what the taste actually is, all you can do is to offer me a bite.

However, if we cannot describe clarity, we certainly can define and measure *unclarity*. We can for example measure the degree of colour or the number of particles per cubic millimetre in a piece of glass. What we have to do is to detect them. Exactly the same applies to mind; Zen training consists in *detecting unclarities of mind, the illusions that we all carry about with us which distort our perception of reality, and in eliminating them.* We want, too, to unravel the tricks of mind which we looked at in the last chapter.

The clear mind

Let us see what the mind would be like if it were perfectly clear. It would be like a perfectly polished mirror, free of distortion and dust, which reflects everything totally and *just as it is.* It would reflect all outside events and also those within, that is to say the mental events of thoughts, feelings and emotions. Everything would be reflected in an equal way, without giving preference to something because it is considered beautiful as opposed to ugly, large as opposed to small, colourful as opposed to drab. All things would be reflected equitably as they are, so that the clear mind can accept all things and persons equally, without preference or prejudice and without value judgements.

But now we come to a crucial point. For accepting things in this way does *not* mean being indifferent, having no values, making no selections. Let us change our analogy to that of a camera. If it has a coloured filter in front of the lens, then only light of that colour will pass into it; or if the film has previous images on it, then the new one will be muddled with them. But if there is no filter and no double exposure, then, when the film is developed we can select or highlight parts of it and remove what we do not want; the preferences and value judgements can now be applied to a perfect image rather than to one which was full of errors and distortions. We must start by having a perfect image on the film – and in our mind. The exposure – the combination of shutter speed and aperture – must be correct for this.

Question: What corresponds to correct exposure in the mind?

A 'perfect image' shows every thing and every person that it contains in its uniqueness, rather than making a generalisation from a somewhat blurred outline. If we go back to the example in Chapter 1 of the manager having an interview with his boss, you will remember that we spoke of his having a fixed idea or image of himself which he was determined to project. It is equally possible to have a fixed image of the boss, but equally ineffective. The 'boss' of whom you have constructed an image based on your previous experience does not correspond exactly to the man or woman you see sitting at a desk as you open the door. There is, in fact, a degree of uncertainty, which must be accepted. If you only have a limited sense of what is, based on what there previously was, you are freezing reality into the past. And you are limiting your freedom of action.

In other words, the clear mind is able to respond to each thing and person in the manner appropriate in every circumstance, in accord with the demand or need that the situation presents. This is because it does not cling on to either a fixed image of itself or hold on to beliefs, preferences and generalisations about others when these are no longer appropriate, for it is constantly alert to the fact that they may at any moment have to be scrapped or modified. For example: two men are at a party. One says to the other,' Do you see those two beautiful women over there? Well, one is my wife and the other is my girlfriend.' 'Funny you should say that,' replies his friend, 'I was just going to say the same thing myself!'

Exercise: Put yourself in the position of the first man. How will you respond to this situation, in which your self-image of a man who has both a faithful wife and a girlfriend has vanished? Try and think of real-life situations in both your business and private life which you have misjudged on the basis of what you previously knew and thought, and in which you might have done better had you been more open to what was actually happening.

We already have what we need

The mind that is *perfectly* clear is 'enlightened', but this state is hardly one we can expect to attain (at least not for the time being!). There is a saying (Winston Churchill) that, 'It would be a pity if nothing were done because not everything can be done', but there is a great deal to be gained even from going part of the way. What is more, throughout the ages the Zen Masters have been telling us that the 'enlightened mind' is actually present in all of us – they refer to it as 'original mind', 'true nature' and in many other ways. All of them show us that no special powers are needed – all we have to do is to recognise what we are.

If we have spoken of Zen so far as being clarity, it is also freedom – another word which cannot be defined. What we mean, what I am trying to convey, is not so much the relative freedom of which we usually speak, the 'freedom of the citizen in a democracy', which is limited, that is to say relative, but the only absolute freedom which exists, freedom of mind. Daisetz Suzuki wrote:

> In its essence, Zen is the art of recognising one's own being. It shows us the way from captivity to freedom . . . We could say that Zen sets all the energies free which are stored within us, but which under normal circumstances are inhibited or distorted, so that we cannot find access to activity . . . It is therefore the object of Zen to keep us from going crazy or becoming cripples. That is what I mean by freedom, to give space for all the creative and benevolent impulses which originate in our hearts. Generally we are blind to the fact that we all possess the necessary abilities to make us happy and love one another.[2]

Clearly, Zen is not a distant, magical or vague vision, but what Master Nansen described as 'everyday mind'. For the wonder of Zen lies in its *pure normality* – that of ourselves and the world. A modern Zen Master is said to have been asked what it was like to have 'satori'. 'Oh,' he said, 'one just walks normally, but an inch above the ground!' There is nothing exceptional about the manager who 'has Zen', he is indistinguishable from all those around him – except that he is freer within himself, more effective – and therefore more successful. And Zen is present in all of us, managers included; all we have to do is to discover its reality.

Know the smallest things and the biggest things, the shallowest and the deepest.

Chapter 3

The Way of Action

> There are various Ways. There is the Way of Salvation by the Law of Buddha, the Way of Confucius governing the Way of Learning, the Way of Healing as a doctor, as a poet teaching the Way of *waka* [a type of poem], tea, archery, and many arts and skills. Each man practises as he feels inclined.
>
> *Miyamoto Musashi*[1]

Miyamoto Musashi was a Samurai (member of the warrior caste) who lived in Japan in the seventeenth century, and one of the greatest, if not the greatest masters of Kendo, the Way of the Sword. This Way is the moral teaching of the Samurai, for to train in Kendo is to subjugate the self, endure gruelling practice and cultivate a level mind in the face of peril. Hand in hand with this martial training goes Zen, which aims directly at the true nature of things. In their essence, all Ways of Zen are the same in this, as we see in the life of Musashi, for not only was he a swordsman, but also a master of arts and crafts, producing masterpieces of ink painting which are perhaps more highly valued in Japan than those of any other. He was a fine calligrapher and sculptor and is said to have written poems and songs. But for us, the greatest interest is to be found in his *A Book of Five Rings*.

'On Wall Street, when Musashi talks, people listen' was the comment of *Time* magazine on Musashi's classic, best-selling guide to strategy. It is a book which lies on the desks of many western managers. On the surface it provides strategy for decision not only on the battlefield, but also in the boardroom, which no doubt accounts largely for its popularity, particularly as it deals with the strategy of warfare and the methods of single combat in exactly the same way – an ideal combination for Wall Street! But when we look more deeply at it, the book is not so much a thesis on strategy as, in Musashi's words, 'a guide for men who want to learn strategy'. And Musashi sees strategy not simply as a means of winning wars and battles, but tells us for example that there is the Way of the farmer; using agricultural instruments he sees the spring through to the autumn with an eye on the changes of the seasons. The Way of the merchant is always to live by taking profit. And he speaks directly to managers:

> The foreman carpenter must know the architectural theory of towers and temples, and the plans of palaces, and must employ men to raise up houses . . . [He] allots his men work according to their ability... If the foreman knows and deploys his work well the finished work will be good. . . . [He] should take into account the abilities and limitations of his men, circulating among them and asking nothing unreasonable. He should know their morale and spirit, and encourage them when necessary. This is the same as the principle of strategy.[2]

And how do we learn strategy, the strategy which is essential to us, not only as managers, but as individuals? Musashi is very clear:

> This is the Way for men who want to learn my strategy:
> 1. Do not think dishonestly.
> 2. The Way is in training.
> 3. Become acquainted with every art.
> 4. Know the Ways of all professions.
> 5. Distinguish between gain and loss in worldly matters.
> 6. Develop intuitive judgement and understanding.
> 7. Perceive things which cannot be seen.
> 8. Pay attention even to trifles.
> 9. Do nothing which is of no use.
>
> It is important to start by setting these broad principles in your heart, and train in the Way of Strategy.[3]

Since the word got around that Japanese managers oriented their strategies according to Musashi's insights, the interest in them in the west is not surprising, for how many Western managers have not been confronted in one way or another with Japanese products? Even if not facing competition from them in his own markets, the average western manager has at least a few Japanese products in office and home – and may well drive a Japanese car. That the success of Japanese industry is one of the most outstanding economic phenomena of our time scarcely needs to be pointed out – and Zen, as expressed in the Way of the Sword and in a great many other ways, has played a great part in it.

How was this amazing feat achieved? Many of the influences which formed the characteristics and structure of present-day Japanese industry originated in the village communities. Even until a hundred years ago, as many as 80 percent of all Japanese were farmers, mostly growing rice, the cultivation of which demanded a high degree of skill and harmonious social organisation. A leading Japanese management consultant has described it thus:

> The rice grows in irrigated fields, mostly on terraced hills. As the lowest fields must receive exactly the same amount of

water as the highest, collaboration between the farmers is essential. The individual cannot carry out his work independently, and because all are very poor, no family can manage without the help of the others. The community therefore needed to work together in providing water reserves, regulating streams and making repairs to fields damaged by typhoons or cloudbursts. This mutual help bordered on strict discipline, and so over a long period a collective consciousness developed, which is still dominant in the Japan of today. Organisation within the group, accepting one's place within the hierarchy and identification with the community are still very much characteristics of the Japanese mentality today, in particular of industrial enterprises. And these are extremely rationally structured machines for production and sales.

Dive headfirst into worldly activity

But this alone would not account for the success of Japanese industry; without the willingness of the individual to devote himself or herself to the achievement of a very high performance and of the best possible results within the group, no such success would be possible. This quality of the *individual,* an unswerving dedication to work, is exemplified by Musashi, who was concerned only with perfecting his skill. And this is part of the cultural background. Equally it is the spirit of Zen Buddhism, in which are concentrated certain principles of Japanese culture which are generally not otherwise expressed. Those acquainted with the history of this culture have discovered counterparts to Zen Buddhism in Protestant ethics, in which the famous sociologist Max Weber saw the roots of western capitalism and the industrial revolution. In the spiritual sense, one of the most important founders of Japanese capitalism was Soshan Suzuki, a Zen monk who was a contemporary of Musashi. He preached self-realisation and perfection through *practical activity* – not, be it noted, through years of sitting in silent meditation.[4] He developed the foundations of an attitude to asceticism in which the renunciation of consumption and the preference for investment were combined in a work-ethic. Its characteristics corresponded to those of the Protestant work-ethic which Max Weber found to be so important. Soshan gave a merchant the following advice over 300 years ago – a Japanese sales director of today might well give the same advice to his departmental managers!

> Dive headfirst into worldly activity. Send your products into other provinces and bring what they produce into your homeland. Travel to the furthest regions of the country, to bring the people there what they want. Your business activity is a kind of asceticism which will free you of all impurities. When the ship sets its sails for the high seas, devote yourself to praying to Buddha. When you understand that this life is only a journey through a changing world, then Heaven will protect you and your profits will be extraordinary. You will become a man of fortune and virtue, yet riches will not impair your nature.

Here we see indeed unconditional dedication to the matter in hand, zealousness to learn, and striving for perfection, all of which are the legacy of Zen Buddhism in Japanese culture. We see also a marked consciousness of the changing nature of the world, which is a fundamental principle of Buddhism – and also an absolute necessity for successful marketing. Here we have the basis of the strategies which have enabled Japanese industry to become so dominant in world trade. As the manager of a subsidiary of a German company in Japan described it, 'The strength of the Japanese is that they concentrate exactly on the main point like a laser beam, with a relatively narrow product programme in a relatively narrow market. And within these narrow markets they concentrate even further on well-defined locations.'

The five rings

Musashi shows the Way of Strategy in five aspects, Ground, Water, Fire, Wind and Void. Bearing in mind that his book is a guide to *learning strategy*, rather than strategy itself, it goes, like any guide, beyond the immediate understanding of the student. The more one reads it, the more one finds in it. What follows is based on his own description of each of the five 'Rings', and as an exercise, it is worth spending time reflecting on each of them.

Ground

This explains the body of the Way of Strategy from the point of view of Musashi's Ichi school (of swordsmanship). 'It is difficult to realise the true Way just through sword-fencing. Know the smallest things and the biggest things, the shallowest things and the deepest things. As if it were a straight road mapped out on the ground, the first book is called the Ground book.' And so it is difficult to realise the true Way just through management. It must be realised in every aspect in one's life, even in the smallest things. As we shall see later, this is an essential part of our Zen training – 24 hours a day, seven days a week!

Water

> With water as the basis, the spirit becomes like water. Water adopts the shape of its receptacle, it is sometimes a trickle and sometimes a wild sea. Water has a clear blue colour. By its clarity, things of Ichi school are shown . . . The strategist makes small things into big things, like building a great Buddha from a one-foot model. I cannot write in detail how this is done. The principle of strategy is having one thing, to know ten thousand things.

The spirit that is like water is like Cook Ting's knife, which can enter where there is no space. It is flexible and adapts itself to all circumstances. This is the quality of effectiveness which enables the manager to cope with ever-changing situations.

Fire

This book is about fighting. The spirit of fire is fierce, whether the fire be small or big, and so it is with battles. The Way of battles is the same for man-to-man fights and ten-thousand-a-side battles . . . What is big is easy to perceive; what is small is difficult to perceive. In short, it is difficult for large numbers of men to change position, so their movements can easily be predicted. An individual can easily change his mind, so his movements are difficult to predict. The essence of this book is that you must train day and night in order to make quick decisions. In strategy it is necessary to treat training as part of normal life with your spirit unchanging.

Wind

The Japanese character for this also means 'tradition'. Musashi explains old, present-day and also family traditions, and says it is difficult to know yourself if you do not know others. But,

> To all Ways there are side-tracks. If you study a Way daily, and your spirit diverges, you may think you are following a good Way, but objectively it is not the true Way. If you are following the true Way and diverge a little, this will later become a large divergence. You must realise this.

Void

By Void I mean that which has no beginning and no end. Attaining this principle means not attaining the principle. The Way of strategy is the Way of nature. When you appreciate the power of nature, knowing the rhythm of any situation, you will be able to hit the enemy naturally and strike naturally. All this is the Way of the Void.

We have already met the Void in Chapter 1, where *wu-wei* was discussed.[5] It means attainment without striving to attain, so that we can, just as did Cook Ting, 'go along with the natural make-up'. The natural make-up is, above all, that of ourselves. And by appreciating the rhythm of the situation, both outside and of ourselves, we can act according to that make-up.

The everyday mind in action

By another great swordsman, a contemporary of Musashi, we are told that the mind which is no-mind is the final stage in swordplay. By 'being of no mind' he means 'everyday mind'. At the beginning of our training, we naturally try to handle the sword as well as possible, just as in any other art, and we must master the technique. However, to quote Daisetz Suzuki:

> But as soon as his mind is fixed on anything, for instance if he desires to do well, or to display his skill, or to excel others, or if he is too anxiously bent on mastering his art, he is sure to commit more mistakes than are actually necessary. Why? Because his self-consciousness or ego-consciousness is too conspicuously present over the entire range of his attention – which in fact interferes with a free display of whatever proficiency he has so far acquired or is going to acquire. He must . . . apply himself to the work to be done as if nothing particular were taking place at the moment . . . He has no feeling of doing anything specially good or bad, important or trivial; it is as if he hears a sound, turns around, and finds a bird in the court. This is one's 'everyday mind'.[6]

Practice: There is a great deal in this chapter on which to reflect. Try to consider whether you always act with your 'everyday mind'. Or are there times when you are *self*-conscious, that is when you are, for example, trying to make a certain impression? Or when you feel that what you are doing is so important that this thought actually hampers you? As always, think of specific occasions – this is far better than trying to see 'what kind of person you are'. Do not go in for so-called 'personality analysis', which is thoroughly misleading. For after all, *what kind of personality makes the analysis?*. You end up in a vicious circle. Much in this book is concerned with emerging from, or very much better, avoiding such circles.

Do you know how to look at a flower?

Chapter 4

The Way of Sincerity

Every morning Zen Master Zuigan Shigen would call out, 'Are you there, Master?' and would reply to himself, 'Yes!' 'Are you awake?' 'Indeed.' 'Do not be fooled by anyone, any time.' 'No I will not.'

Mumonkan[1]

. . . to thine own self be true,
And it must follow, as the night the day,
Thou canst not then be false to any man.

Shakespeare[2]

The true value of the art of management cannot be seen within the confines of management technique. It is only to be found in the whole person, the person who, as we said earlier, puts on his business suit and tie ready to play his role as manager. But it is very easy to fool oneself about this. The manager's work as an individual, unless he or she is right at the top (perhaps even then), is but one small input amongst the many which make up the final product. But, for his own sense of self-esteem, he often finds it necessary play a role which he regards as worthy of himself. It has sometimes amused me to observe this at a management meeting, where people introduce and defer to each other by position (Director of Manufacturing, Chief Accountant and so on) without any real knowledge of the content or quality of each other's work. Thus, it is less what a person does and more what he or she appears to do which has become the basis for judging competence.

Question: How do you judge *your own* competence? Do you fool yourself? Are you an effective person – or just a manager? Be honest – there's no one else around!

Looking at a flower

To answer these questions, it is necessary to know how to look at oneself. Or how to look at *anything,* for that matter, in the sense of doing so with clarity. For example, do you know how to look at a flower? Most people do not. They stand away from it and never grasp its spirit. It is as if they are dreaming of a flower. For most people, subject and object are separated by an unbridgeable gap, and there is no grasping of the actual facts before them. Now it might be thought that the answer of Zen to this would be to give a 'sense of oneness', of identification with the flower, and in this to find not 'the restless movement on the surface of life but the eternal tranquillity seen through and beyond change'.[3] In no way is this Zen.

What we are trying to get closer to here is the real significance of what was said in the Introduction, 'In the face of chaos, Zen maintains peace of mind.' First of all, Zen is not an experience of identity with the world, with nature, nor is it a feeling of eternal tranquillity. Why not a sense of identity? Or even 'oneness with the cosmos', a fashionable term which has its origin in Freud and Hinduism (Yoga)? If you watch a young child playing with a toy, you will see no 'sense of identity', but complete absorption in the toy *as it really is*. The child deals directly with the toy, and we cannot speak of any intervening concept of identification. In fact, any concept which is set up to explain the facts of experience of the child *only serves to obscure them*, and always ends in creating complexities and confusion.

If we speak of an identification between subject and object, we presuppose that there was originally an opposition, a separation between them. Zen, however (with a logic that is sometimes devastatingly direct), says that the opposition, the separation, was never real, but is only created by the attempt of thought to analyse the situation. Therefore it aims to restore the original experience of clarity and non-separateness, that which the child has.

If the *sense* of identity, but not the *fact* of it, is foreign to Zen, what of tranquillity? Nature is always in motion, never at a standstill, and therefore we must catch it in motion. But there is a paradox here. Remembering the 'tranquillity beneath the restless movement of life', which so many seek, imagine you are looking at the still waters of a canal. The tranquillity is on the surface; but below it, all is restless movement! Tranquillity and motion are, then, only two aspects of the same whole, and so as long as we seek one without the other we are artificially creating a barrier dividing nature into two parts – they are irreconcilable, and we stumble into paradox. To seek only for tranquillity is to kill nature and there is nothing left but the dead corpse of abstraction. When we, however,succeed in breaking down the barriers, then we can see into the living heart of nature and live with it *as it really is.*

The effects of eliminating the barriers, not only between ourselves and reality, *and the barriers within ourselves*, are profound. Here for example is a dialogue between Master Ummon and a monk:

Monk: What is the pure body of truth?
Master: The hedgerow.

Monk: What is the behaviour of one who understands in this way?
Master: He is a golden-haired lion.[4]

You may ask what a hedgerow has to do with a lion. Ummon is simply pointing to facts of experience and saying, *'Look!'*, and the hedgerow, near which they were surely standing, was just a convenient object of experience at that moment. And to continue with another Master:

> Monk: It is said that when a lion seizes upon his opponent he uses his power to the utmost. Pray tell me what this power is.
> Master: The spirit of sincerity.

Sincerity, in literal translation from the Japanese means 'the power of not deceiving'. As Master Rinzai explained it, it is:

> The whole being in action, in which nothing is kept in reserve, nothing disguised, nothing goes to waste. When a person lives like this he is said to be a golden-haired lion; he is the symbol of virility, sincerity and whole-heartedness; he is divinely human; he is not a manifestation but reality itself, for he has nothing behind him, he is the whole truth, the very thing.[5]

Why am I a manager?

If in some measure you have from this come to appreciate the spirit of sincerity and are prepared to be absolutely honest with yourself, you may be able to answer this question. Or at least you will realise the importance of doing so. In effect, what you will be doing as you struggle with this – and it is indeed a struggle – you will be stripping away a series of masks, one inside the other. *Do not reject any answer because you do not like what you find, or because it is something you would never admit even to your closest friend.* If, just for example, the answer is 'because I like to have power over other people, I enjoy controlling them', look at this in exactly the way you would an answer which is more socially acceptable; do not make any value judgements at this stage.

The real value of this exercise lies in the fact that you will almost certainly fail! You will discover that you cannot adopt neutral attitudes to your own motives, that you filter many things out before you really examine them. As in our earlier analogy of a camera, the mind is not getting all of the image. It is fooling itself – and that is really what Master Shigen at the beginning of this chapter was talking about.

Your failure will have show you that you do not know how to look at yourself – and therefore also you have not really learned how to look at the world: in a word, you *do not see things as they really are.* The next part of this book is devoted to developing just this ability.

On the ethical level

As a tailpiece to this chapter, something should be said of the ethics involved. Because Zen asks, even demands, that one should look at oneself – and one's motives – without any positive or negative attitude to them, it might be thought to be entirely unprincipled, accepting everything. This, however, is certainly not so. For once the truth about oneself has been recognised, then one's real nature is free – and the underlying recognition of Zen is that this is good, and that it is only hidden and unable to express itself because we fool ourselves. If, on the other hand, you believe that mankind's basic nature is evil – then Zen is not for you.

PART 2 – OPENING THE MIND

Who does not want to improve the quality of his attention to the matter in hand?

Chapter 5

The Way of Mindfulness[1]

When mind is comprehended, all is comprehended.
The Buddha

We now come to the hardest part of the book, for this is where the real work begins. In it a programme of training is recommended, and an effort of will is needed to carry this out, not just a few times as a novelty, but over a long period. Do not expect immediate results, any more than you would in training for sport. It may be that you do not at first understand some of the explanations given; if so, the best thing to do is to try the exercises and practices themselves, for, as is so often the case if we look at the history of civilisation, theory often comes *after practice*.

The chapter has two sections. In the first we are concerned with discovering how the mind works and with **bare attention**, which is the method of obtaining that clarity of which we spoke in Chapter 2. In the second section, we look at **clear comprehension,** a term which speaks for itself. At the end of the first section details of training practice are given, and it is advisable to gain at least a certain amount of experience with this before going further. Naturally, you could continue immediately if you want to get a global view first, but if you do this you should then return to this point and practise bare attention.

Mindfulness through bare attention

What is mindfulness?

'Mindfulness' is perhaps a word we do not often use, but is of special importance to us here. Usually we speak of being mindful of something in the sense of remembering it; 'be mindful that there is a speed limit on this road', for example. But in the context of Zen training it refers not to the past but to the present, and as a general term it carries the meanings of both 'attention' and 'awareness', together with composure. This gives us the most accurate and perfect description of Zen *composed awareness*. Look at the cat at the beginning of this Chapter! It is relaxed, alert and ready for anything which may happen.

Most people think that the mind should be filled with as many things as possible, for after all that is the aim of our educational system. But there is a story about a professor who visited a Zen Master, who, as is the custom, offered him tea. The professor held out his cup and the Master went on pouring and pouring. The professor watched silently, but eventually could not refrain from saying, 'It's full, no more will go in.' 'Just so,' said the master. 'you are also full, with all your opinions and speculations. How can I show you Zen until you have emptied your cup?'

The more the mind is filled with its own ideas and concepts, the less sensitive and receptive it is to those of others and – note this – *to its own creative ideas*.

Mindfulness takes things with uncertainty, rather than having a limited and prejudged sense of what is. Take for example that you meet someone today who was in a foul temper yesterday. If you have 'frozen' yesterday's image into your mind, you may overlook the fact that the person is today full of the joys of spring. In other words, you are open to the individuality of all people and things, you are not fixed into static generalisations.

Mindfulness is, then, *skilful attentiveness,* an aspect of Zen that will surely appeal to all managers, for who does not want to improve the quality of his attention to the matter in hand, and to be able to maintain this, not just in moments of strenuous concentration, but to let it be the natural and *relaxed* state of mind all the time? The manager who has cultivated mindfulness carries out all the various aspects of his work in a harmonious way. Not only does he act calmly in hectic situations, but does not stress himself unnecessarily when strong concentration is needed. *He maintains a balance between relaxation and effort.* More than this, mindfulness is an essential quality in dealing with other people – which is, after all, a great part of a manager's work. Mindfulness, through its aspects of bare attention and clear comprehension, leads to awareness and understanding of people. One might say that the cultivation of mindfulness is not only cultivation of the intellect, but also of the heart.

The training in actual practice

We now come to the practical business of discovering our Zen, for that is what all Zen training is concerned with. We want to discover it not as something special, something apart from our daily life, but within it. This is the object of all Zen training. The swordfighter discovers it in his training *as a swordfighter,* the artist in his painting and the Zen monk in his daily routine of meditation, work in the fields or around the temple, in fact during every moment of the day. And the manager? He too can discover Zen in his daily life, from the moment he wakes to the time he goes to sleep. This is not a matter of 'practising Zen', for that would be quite impossible; you cannot simply sit down and 'do Zen', for it is inseparable from 'ordinary' living.

But still, training is needed, is indeed essential. This resembles the training sessions which a tennis player, for instance, carries out daily, practising strokes under the guidance of the trainer, *and then using them in the game itself* becoming more proficient in their use until they become part of a natural way of playing. In the same way, Zen will become part of your being and functioning as a manager, because it will have become active in your being as a whole.

The 'training' sessions are absolutely necessary. How much time you spend on them, where and when, are entirely up to you, but I would suggest half an hour a day regularly – I would not ask more of a busy manager. Try if possible to find a quiet place where you are not disturbed and can relax; no special sitting position is necessary – experiment until you discover what brings the best results. But make sure that you do not fall asleep . . .

The process of discovering Zen is not one of discovering anything new or special – this cannot be said too often. It is our natural way of being; therefore it would be better to speak of 'uncovering' our Zen, and this is exactly what we are going to do, by investigating what covers it up, what prevents it from expressing itself. This is a quite scientific process, and so we first need to examine how the mind works. Here I want to emphasize that you will make no fresh discoveries in this, and paradoxically, everything you are going to find out about your mind is something that you actually know already. As was said in the Introduction, Zen is blindingly obvious. But how often do we overlook the obvious?

Question: Have you ever before now tried to discover how your mind works? I do not mean, have you ever studied psychology, but have you ever observed your own mind *in action* and seen what tricks it plays on you?

The mind is a mirror

What is the nature of mind? We are not going into metaphysics here, we are not trying to solve the famous 'mind-body problem' or speculating about the nature of existence. Instead we are asking what the mind *does* and how it functions. It is a dynamic mechanism, reflecting, recording and recalling the impressions we receive from outside ourselves through our senses, and also from 'inside' – we can in fact speak of a 'mind-sense' here. And within this mirror-mind, thoughts and feelings come and go, appearing, vanishing and reappearing in response to circumstances.

Exercise: Pause for a while in your reading, close your eyes and without concentrating on anything in particular, notice how thoughts, images and feelings come and go. Each one comes into the mind, stays for a while and then is replaced by another. The mind is 'freewheeling'. Note how anything that happens such as hearing a sound from outside, instantly brings a fresh thought into the mind; you become *conscious* of the sound. The process of *attention* is beginning.

Let us look at this more closely. When an object, whether it be an external one detected by one of the five physical senses or an internal one detected by the mind-sense, presents itself to the mind, attention is aroused and consciousness of it comes into being. Without this there would be no perception of any object at all. But this is only the first phase of the process of perception, and it results only in a very general and indistinct picture of the object. You can easily verify that this is so.

Exercise: What can you remember of the sound you heard just a few minutes ago? How loud was it, how long did it last? Or, to take another example, how much do you actually register about a car which you overtake while driving? Certainly you are conscious of it and take care not to collide with it, but you only have a very general picture of it – usually you do not even notice what make of car or what colour it is. Think of other types of situation where this happens: what colour shoes was your secretary wearing today? She certainly had shoes on, and your eyes were very probably directed towards them for at least a moment, but . . .

It would of course be quite intolerable if the mind did not work in this way, for the amount of information presented to it in every moment is enormous, and therefore a selection process takes place. If the impression of the object is strong enough, or if you are interested in it, your attention is more closely directed towards it and you begin to notice details. The attention then begins not only to notice various characteristics of the object, but also – this is a critical point – *the relationship of the object to yourself.*

Exercise: Before you read further, consider what kinds of relationship may exist here. If the 'object' is a pin stuck into your arm, immediately followed by a pain, you feel dislike for it. If your partner comes into the room, you may have a positive reaction – or a negative one because you have been interrupted in your reading! In each case, the relationship between you and the object is at least slightly coloured, it is not that of a neutral observer. You will be able to think of countless situations in which there is this colouration of your perception – *indeed it will be rather difficult to discover a situation where this does not happen.* After all, how often are we really impartial?

Because the attention has now directed itself not only to the object but also to its relationship with *you*, the mind starts comparing the present perception with similar ones from the past; the experiences of present and past are co-ordinated. If this did not happen, all that the attention could accomplish would be merely to collect isolated facts. What we see here is what is called 'associative thinking'; the final stage of the development of attention is the generalisation of the experience. From this stage the mind moves to that of abstract thinking.

The source of our difficulties

What we want to ask now is, *how reliable is this thinking process?* It is an important question, because by far the greatest part of our mental life takes place in this way. To summarise so far, the mind progresses from initial attention to interest and increase of detail in perception, then makes reference to the observer and begins associative and finally abstract thinking. This entire process takes place in a very wide field, from the close observation of everyday facts to research work and the subtleties of philosophy. But however much it may achieve, the process contains a *built-in potential for error*, and here is the source of a great deal of our trouble.

The problem begins at the point where the mind makes reference to the observer, that is to itself. But surely, you will say, this sounds somewhat familiar, for it is the question of whether a scientific observation can in actual fact be independent of the observer. In the case of the untrained mind, certainly not. For directly the mind begins associative thinking a connection is made between the immediate perception of the object and objects from the past, and therefore the present perception is coloured by previous ones.

Exercise: Look for a moment at any object and notice how you immediately associate it with similar ones. For example if you look in a particular direction and see a rectangular hole in the wall filled in with glass and framed in wood, and through this a patch of sky, the word 'window' will at once come into your mind – you have now associated the hole in the wall with windows you have previously seen. Actually, of course, you could very well have been looking at a cleverly done painting! Try and find other similar examples by looking round you in the room you are in now. Watch the association process at work.

However, the associative process goes further than this. Not only may you make a wrong association with the object you have perceived, but also there may be – almost certainly there will be – an admixture of emotional and intellectual preferences, wishful thinking and so on. You might dispute this, and say that you are perfectly capable of looking at things in an unprejudiced way and quite dispassionately. But consider; as soon as you have made any association between the object presented to you and the emotions or prejudices which arise in connection with it, and then move on to another object, the first one goes back into your memory *together with all the new associations you have made*. The next time a similar object presents itself, the first one re-emerges as before – but now together with the judgements, emotions, decisions and moods which it has 'collected'.

I do not like making an analogy between the human mind and a computer, but if to do so helps you to understand what has been said, go ahead and work it out. You could even draw a diagram.

Exercise: I realise that this explanation of the mind-process is perhaps a little complex, and in any case it occurs so quickly that it is difficult to observe. But take for example the case where you had a bad meal in a restaurant. The next time you pass that way you remember the unpleasant meal and a feeling of dislike – let us hope, not disgust – arises. Fine, but maybe they have a new cook now . . . Once again, try to find your own examples.

Training in bare attention

We now come to one of the most important aspects of Zen

training, as explained by one of the most renowned and scholarly European Buddhist monks, Venerable Nyanaponika:

> Bare Attention is the clear and single-minded awareness of what actually happens *to* us and *in* us. It is called 'bare', because it attended just to the bare facts of a perception as presented either through the five physical senses or the mind... When attending to that six-fold sense-impression, attention or mindfulness is kept to a bare registering of the facts observed, without reacting to them by deed, speech or by mental comment, which may be one of self-reference (like, dislike, etc.), judgement or reflection.[2]

This, to put it mildly, does not seem a very easy thing to do. In the normal way, we are not concerned with a disinterested judgement of things, but with 'handling' and judging them from our own point of view. We put labels on the things which form our mental and physical world, and these mostly show our self-interest, and restrict our vision. We live in an assemblage of labels, and these determine first our reactions, and then our actions. We can see this very clearly when we look at our dealings with other people.

Exercise: Can you think of examples where you attach labels to people, to your boss, to your colleagues, or to your partner perhaps? At this stage, just take a note of the facts.

The importance and value of bare attention is that it allows things – *and people* – to speak for themselves, without being interrupted by our own judgements and reactions. On the one hand it gives them a chance to finish what they are saying. And on the other it allows us to listen to them without being deafened by the noise and confusion of our own thoughts and the hustle and bustle going on around us. Therefore it is continually revealing a great deal that is new to us, things which we have never noticed before. Bare attention opens the mind and allows us to see with clarity – and now you will begin to see how the clarity of which we spoke in Chapter 2 can actually be brought about. Bare attention opens wider horizons to us, thus obtaining, apparently without any effort, results which no amount of intellectual straining could achieve.

Practising bare attention. It is time now to find out for yourself whether there is any reality in what I have been saying, and therefore bare attention should become the subject of your daily training sessions. It is not as difficult as it sounds. During the half-hour you have hopefully been able to set aside for this (it could be less, but twenty minutes is really the minimum) sit comfortably relaxed in a fairly upright chair, but not allowing your back to slump.

Close your eyes and try to feel the movement of your breath through your nostrils, but do not attempt to follow the movement of the breath down through the body. OK, you can feel the breath? Yes, *but only for a few moments.* Why? because some thought or other has come into your mind, you have heard a sound or perhaps become aware of some feeling. Don't worry, this is quite normal, this is what happens to us all the time. Do not try to push the thought (or feeling) away with the idea 'I must concentrate on my breath', but instead, *just notice the thought which came.* After a short while the thought will disappear, and you can pay attention to the feeling of your breath again. And so you go on. Each time a thought appears, or when you hear a sound, or you feel a pain or an itch, look at it as though it was a bird flying past, and when it has gone, go back to the breath.

And that is all there is to it. Bare attention consists simply in actually noticing what is happening, in becoming aware in a way which we do not normally do. Most particularly, you will become aware, as you practise, of the way your mind is working: you will come to understand the mechanism of your emotions and feelings and how they affect your reasoning power, the true and pretended motives for your actions and many other aspects of your mental life.

Bare attention in daily life

Bare attention is not something which we can sustain throughout our ordinary life, apart from the daily training sessions. Not only have we got too much to do, but since the mind constantly needs to define its position in regard to itself and the outer world, and we must continually choose, decide, judge and finally act, we cannot live in a state of continual detachment. And yet, by stepping back from people and things from time to time, the tensions which so often arise from unnecessary interference and from our likes and dislikes and other kinds of self-reference are relaxed, and so we are no longer troubled by them.

There are two further possibilties of putting bare attention into practice. One is, to do such small tasks as washing, and brushing the teeth, with this attitude, *taking notice of what is going on*: feeling the brush moving over the teeth, etc. One thing you will find in this case is that automatically you will brush your teeth more carefully and thoroughly – because you will not be thinking of something else at the same time. You might think also of using bare attention in other activities, such as eating and walking (see below).

The second possibility is to try to spend a day or perhaps a weekend in the attitude of bare attention, just being aware of everything that is happening, including your own reactions. Of course there will often be times when bare attention 'slips'. In this case the thing to do is quite simply to notice that that happened – and continue. This is no bad thing, for you may become aware of *why* you let your attention go.

An alternative method of practice: You might like to try a different method of practising bare attention during your training sessions – slow walking, or *Kin-Hin* as it is called. Clasp you hands lightly together on your breast or let them hang loosely by your sides. Shrug your shoulders a few times to make sure they are relaxed, then begin to walk *as slowly as you possibly can*; the movements of the feet should be scarcely discernible. Do not watch them, but look somewhat ahead of you. There is nothing special to concentrate on, except to walk as slowly as possible. Twenty minutes of this has a remarkable effect; it is a very good practice.

Mindfulness through clear comprehension

In contrast to the passively receptive attitude of bare attention, clear comprehension focuses on the active part of our lives, that which occupies the greater part of our time. But here there is a trap which an active, busy manager who wants to increase his effectiveness might easily fall into. It is impossible to cultivate and apply clear comprehension without having a sound basis of bare attention. You can see this even before we have begun to discuss clear comprehension in detail, for how can you truly understand anything unless you have first carefully observed and studied it? There is no short-cut here.

Our aim is to make clear comprehension gradually become the regulative force of all our activities, to make them purposeful, efficient and in accordance with the realities of the situation. To the clarity of bare attention is added clear comprehension.

Clear comprehension of purpose

We like to think of ourselves as 'rational beings' who always act 'rationally', but is this really true? The fact of the matter is that even when the purpose we have in mind is quite clear and unmistakable, we often forget it under the pressure of getting things done. We forget our programmes and our principles, not only out of rashness or passion, but through quite casual whims, childish curiosity or just plain laziness.

Now, under the impact of the multiple impressions which constantly bombard us from outside, and the manifold events taking place within us, deviations from our true purposes are unavoidable for most of us. Therefore it is necessary to keep them to a minimum. But this cannot be achieved by an effort of will, however determined, for sooner or later the pressure becomes too great, and there is an emotional reaction which may burst the bounds of rationality.

Question: Can you honestly say that this has never happened to you, that you have never 'broken out', or at any rate felt a strong temptation to do so, even though you resisted it?

One might speak of an area of potential irrational behaviour which is always present in the mind. Within it there is tension which cannot be kept under control, much less eliminated, by force. How can we keep it in check *without creating a further tension for the purpose of holding the first one back?* (You may need to think this one out!)

Let us recall Cook Ting once more. As he cut up his ox, he used no violence, but his knife followed a way which we can now see as 'peaceful penetration'. Therefore his knife never needed sharpening, in contrast to that of the mediocre cook, who had to keep sharpening his knife, because he hacked. *The 'knife' we have now is nothing less than bare attention.* As you may have noticed during your practice with it, it leads to a certain slowing down, a healthy tendency to pause and think for a moment before acting in any way – particularly, I might add, in speech! The pauses – even if they are not noticeable to other people – allow time to consider whether what we are about to do or say is in line with our purpose or not. And bare attention, because it provides reliable data on which to base this judgement, is a quite essential first step to clear comprehension.

Another of the benefits to be obtained by clear comprehension of purpose based on bare attention is that one seems to have more time for everything! This is because instead of being driven here and there by a 'Time Planning System', one checks constantly whether all those dates and appointments one has written down somewhat unthinkingly actually do serve one's real purposes.

To sum this up: clear comprehension of purpose on the one hand saves waste of energy, and on the other concentrates it where it is most effective.

Exercise: Look through your appointments diary for the last two weeks and ask yourself whether everything you did had a valid and useful purpose. How many appointments were made without clear comprehension of purpose? Now go through *next week's* appointments!

Needless to say, clear comprehension of purpose is not restricted to planning time, which I used as an example (a useful one), but applies to all our activities. Or does it?

Clear comprehension of suitability

We are not always such masters of the situation that we can choose that course of action which would be most purposeful, for circumstances often do not permit that and in any case our own capacities have limits; we are concerned with the art of the practicable here. Well, you might say, there is nothing new in this, as a manager I am continually concerned with what is actually achievable. Naturally, no matter what I plan, I must always take the resources available into account. Yes, indeed, but what about your own *inner* resources? How often do you bring these into the equation? If you take them into account, you will save yourself many unnecessary failures, and if a failure does occur, you will be less inclined to attribute it incorrectly to the purpose you set out to achieve or the means you chose – or even to other people.

What, then, are your inner resources? They will certainly include your emotional strengths – and therefore weaknesses! – as well as intellectual and physical abilities. You will discover all these as you train yourself in bare attention, and here is an important point: do not omit your weaknesses! The attitude of bare attention is to observe *without making judgements*, and it is only by doing this that you will be in a position to strengthen yourself where necessary. Since you are, after all, alone with yourself, there is no need to try to hide your weaknesses out of shame. Be honest, or, if you recall the story at the beginning of Chapter 4, 'Do not be fooled by anyone, any time'. Not even by yourself!

To sum up, Zen emerges when mindfulness is present. And mindfulness combines bare attention and clear comprehension.

This chapter may have proved a hard nut to crack. But if the effort of reading it has been worthwhile, then the effort of carrying through the training is infinitely more so. The two modes of practice, bare attention and clear comprehension, supplement each other, for the first develops increased alertness and self-control. And the second makes it considerably easier to guide one's deeds and words, rather than being taken unawares by situations, carried away by one's emotions or misled by deceptive appearances.

And finally, clear comprehension creates a more suitable atmosphere for bare attention, since it brings a controlling and calming influence into the world of never-ceasing action and restless thought. And this is Zen: maintaining inner peace within the external chaos. And the way to it is mindfulness.

Could it be that sometimes we come to the point of making a decision simply because we are tired of thinking?

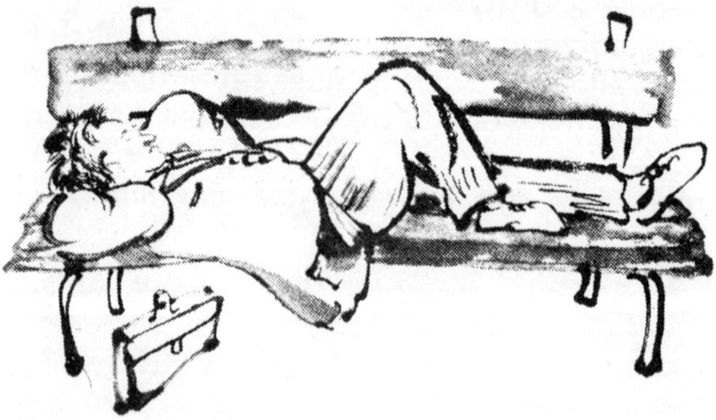

Chapter 6

The Way of Intuition

> People such as master musicians have the music score in front of their noses, or flourish swords in several ways when they have mastered the Way, but that does not mean that they fix their eyes on those things specifically, or that they make pointless movements of the sword. It means that they can see naturally.
>
> 'Perception' and 'sight' are the two different methods of seeing . . . As I said before, if you fix your eyes on details and neglect the important things, your spirit will become confused, and victory will escape you. Research this principle well and train diligently.
>
> *Miyamoto Musashi*[1]

We have discussed two aspects of vision – that is to say, of the vision of the 'mind's eye' – clarity and openness. Now our topic is widening the vision, and we are concerned with intuition.[2] On the whole, this is not a quality held in very high regard by managers, partly because management training emphasises the use of rational, logical techniques almost to the exclusion of other potentially useful skills. And so those managers who do make use of their intuitive abilities need to camouflage this by giving carefully worked-out arguments for decisions they actually made intuitively. And one might add that the sexist idea that women are more 'intuitive' than men often works out to their disadvantage!

If the logical analysis of information believed to be factual was a 100 per cent reliable means of problem-solving and decision-making, life would be a lot easier for managers, for then all the responsibility could be given over to computers. But as it is, the constantly evolving dynamic of change frequently wrecks even the most comprehensive attempts at trend analysis. And so without intuition the world would probably be unworkable, as least as far as managers are concerned. It would also be a much more drab place, lacking both the arts and invention. Take for example the 'Big Mac'.

> If Ray Kroc of McDonald's had listened to expert advice, we might never have become addicted to Big Macs. In 1960 his attorneys advised him against purchasing the McDonald's name. Kroc reportedly closed his office door, cursed, threw things out of the window and then called his attorneys back with orders to buy it anyway. 'I felt in my funny bone it was a sure thing', Kroc said. The price was $2.7 million. McDonald's sales exceeded $4.5 billion by 1978.[3]

The traditional view has always been that intuition is either innate or absent. You either have it or you don't. But in fact we do not need to consider it as rare, for it is a capacity which lies in the human brain, a function of mind which works perfectly naturally if allowed to develop. But most of us do not allow it to develop, for we are schooled and motivated to use only our logical, rational faculty. Therefore the way of Zen is to break down this resistance, to give free space to intuition. But note carefully: intuition is not something we can 'develop', for an intuitive event is something which happens spontaneously.

Exercise: Do something spontaneous *now!* Almost certainly, you can't. Instead you are probably sitting in a half-paralysed state *trying to think of something spontaneous to do!*

It is equally frustrating to try to do something intuitive – intuition never works when we try to force it. What we need to do is to understand it more clearly so that we can learn how to free it, how we can be like Cook Ting, who went about the task of cutting up his ox 'going along with the natural make-up' rather than like the 'mediocre cook, who hacks'.

Left brain, right brain?

It is frequently said that there are two types of thinking, rational and intuitive, and that these are respectively centred in the left and right hemispheres of the brain, and therefore are separate functions. In Chapter 7, 'The way of creativeness', we shall see that this is the *wrong metaphor* for intuition and its outcome, creativity. This is because it does not take into account certain other parts of the brain which have a unifying function. Modern research increasingly bears this out.

As a side-issue here, but a not unimportant one, we are constantly constructing metaphors in order to enable us to deal with the real world. This is helpful, and frequently essential, but on the other hand we are likely to get into trouble when we mistake the metaphor for the real thing or choose the wrong metaphor. This is of course the principle, made famous by Alfred Korzybski, that the map is not the territory and the name is not the thing named. But he was merely repeating what Lao Tzu had said a few thousand years before him, that the Tao which can be named is not the eternal Tao, for the meaning of Tao includes intuition. To return to intuition, the unifying function of mind ensures that it works *as a whole*, at times mainly in the rational mode, at others mainly in the intuitive, but no part of it is ever 'switched off' completely. (Here I disregard the effects of certain drugs or manipulative meditation techniques, which create purely artificial situations which no scientist would claim fully to understand.) Musashi makes this quite clear. The musicians certainly have the music in front of their noses and read the notes – a logical operation – but 'that does not mean that they fix their eyes on them specifically' *and to the exclusion of all else*, the conductor and the other players, for example, for then the result would be confusion accompanied by 'pointless movements of the baton'.

The fact that the mind always works as a whole has remarkable consequences, for it means that even when we think we are being wholly rational, this is not really the case. Intuition is always present, even if we suppress it. We can take as a prime example the matter of *making decisions*, for after all, that is largely what management is about. Most writers on management discuss the technique of making decisions, Peter Drucker for one.[4] But what we want to ask here, is what do such decision-making processes lack – for certainly they do go wrong at times, the disastrous case of the Ford Edsel car being a classic example.[5]

How rational is 'rational'?

When we make a decision we feel that we are acting rationally, and therefore *in accordance with good management principles*. We collect data which seems to us appropriate, analyse it, and then we make projections on which we base a decision. Is this fully justified? Is it actually sufficient? For surely, some very pertinent questions arise:

- How do we really know what information is relevant, since our plans are constantly upset by unforeseen events?
- How do we know when we have collected *enough* information on which to decide? Does the information itself tell us that?

- Is it perhaps the case that we go through the motions of gathering and processing the information in a rational way and then, because time is pressing and the decision can no longer be postponed, we act?
- Could it be that sometimes we come to the point of making a decision simply because we are tired of thinking?

It seems as though the 'rigorously scientific' method of predicting the future – which is, of course, what decisions are about – can be applied only in special cases: where prompt action is not urgent, where the factors involved are largely mechanical or where the circumstances are so restricted as to make the decision trivial. In making major decisions, however, the conditions are quite different: the level of uncertainty is high, there is little precedent, the variables are not scientifically predictable, the 'facts' are limited and do not make it clear which way to go, time is short, and there are several plausible objectives to choose from. Above all, no two situations requiring a decision are ever identical. Therefore all decisions have an intuitive element, whether we are aware of it or not, and so to improve the quality of our decision-making, we must allow intuition to play its part.

Intuition and planning – the middle way

Spontaneity is not by any means a blind, disorderly urge, a mere power of caprice, and it would be a great mistake to suppose that the type of manager who does not believe in planning and deliberation, but instead reacts in panic to every crisis that comes along, is acting with intuition. The mere denial that planning and schedules are ever effective, on the contrary, points to a total lack of intuition, or rather, complete inability to use it to real advantage. This, after all, we have learnt from Musashi, that he does not throw away his years of training and skill – the 'planning' – but knows their value as well as their limitations. One can be spontaneous without being spontaneously foolish!

The opposite pole from complete rejection of planning is that of the fallacy of what the American philosopher Alfred North Whitehead called 'misplaced concreteness'. It cannot be denied that plans and schedules, especially if well documented and presented with fine-looking graphics, have a seductive quality which gives them an air of truth. But in fact they may very well be based on nothing more than a false logic that puts everything in order – except reality!

The middle way of intuition is to prevent preconceived ideas from determining one's course of action and at the same time to filter out unthinking impulses. Outdated plans are of course highly destructive, and all sound managements continually revise their plans *in the light of events*, so that plans are not only ordering events but also being modified by them (as in a sophisticated control-system). This is a process in which the free flow of intuition is vital, for only through this can the new set of assumptions on which the new plan is to be based be made. And so what we see is this: intuition provides a wider perspective from which data can be gathered on which decision can be based. And the actual process of making a decision occurs spontaneously.

Question: Do you have some reservations about this? Do you perhaps think that, even with the wider data base of intuition, all decisions are made 'rationally'? If so: Do something which is *not* spontaneous *now!* How did the thought of the something you were going to do arise? You can only answer – spontaneously!

But please do not try to analyse this any further, for you will only tie yourself up in knots. It is far better simply to accept it. This we have learned from Musashi, but now comes a more personal aspect.

Question: When you yourself have conceived a plan, a strategy or a decision, how much faith do you have in it? Suppose you think that your plan is such a fine product of your own highly trained, experienced mind and so logically conceived that it cannot fail, how far will you commit yourself to it?

The point of this question is that we do take a pride in our plans, in all the hard work we have put into them, and this makes us blind to our own intuition. We are, to go back a few chapters, *fooling ourselves*, and we identify ourselves with the wonderful plan. What is necessary, vital, in fact, is to be able to look at our own ideas with detachment, without being seduced by their surface brilliance, without committing one of the Seven Deadly Sins – pride!

Freeing intuition through mindfulness

Although a great deal has been written about intuition, to attempt to define it is to fall into a trap. It is not simply that intuition and the rational act of definition are of different logical types, but since intuition is what it is precisely because *it does not exist within any logical system*, obviously it cannot be defined by logic. The attempt to do so is like trying to bundle up a 'piece' of water in string. Yet just as we can either stop or release the flow of water, so we can release the flow of intuition.

Following our basic strategy of *knowing, shaping and freeing* the mind, we have already discovered something about the nature of intuition, though what you have learned from my words is, so to speak, only a signpost to intuition. For the next two steps, which actually take place together with the first (it is only for convenience that we speak of them separately), the key is *mindfulness*, in its two aspects of bare attention and clear comprehension. In your training sessions of bare attention you will have noticed how all kinds of thoughts appear in the mirror of the mind and then disappear. It is a quite spontaneous process – you are not attempting to produce a logical sequence. And then, because the attention is *bare*, that is to say *free* from all value judgements such as good or bad, true or false (these are logical types, be it noted), the flow proceeds smoothly, without interruption. Now, even though you do not normally notice it, there is a flow of ideas taking place in the mind all the time. But when you interpose a selection process, when you only admit certain types of thought to full consciousness, then those thoughts which do not fit into your predetermined pattern of thinking are filtered out, rejected as inappropriate.

Where does the flow of thoughts originate? It comes from all our previous experiences and memories of the past – you may have noticed in training that memories of things you had quite 'forgotten' often emerge. And partly from the cues in the present upon which you are not actually concentrating – here we think of Musashi's musicians, who, although they are reading the music with 'sight', are at the same time aware of the conductor, the other players and even the audience with 'perception', the peripheral vision of the mind.

Bare attention, then, gives us access to the intuitive level of the mind. But there is more going on here than a stream of data, impressions and memories, for often there is what one might call a 'pre-decision', and then from the intuitive level a signal comes indicating its presence. We have already had one example, the 'feeling in my funny bone' that Ray Kroc had before he called his attorneys and told them to buy McDonald's. Speaking personally, there are times during my work when I have a feeling that I do not want to write any more but nevertheless I do actually want to continue – the will to work further is present. Well, if I were to dismiss this feeling as mere laziness and force myself to continue, I would be ignoring a vital signal – that what I was writing or *was about to write* was heading in the wrong direction. Usually it is enough to flip back the pages and read again what I have written and then the problem becomes clear, or take a cup of coffee and a look at the newspaper, or in extreme cases even a walk in the park allows the intuitive predecision to become clear. What is more, there is a feeling of relief, even of excitement when this happens, and I cannot wait to get back to the keyboard!

Exercise: Discover what your own signals are and the best ways to attend to them, and where and how you can find even a brief moment for bare attention to the signals. If there is no time, at least make a note of them.

So not only does bare attention give us access to intuition itself, it also allows us to interpret its signals, and this is why its practice is so important. The signals can, of course, be of many kinds apart from feelings in the 'funny bone' or my own laziness. They can go so far as to include anxiety, discomfort, or an upset stomach and sleepless nights, or just a bad mood. If any of these happen, don't blame your colleagues or take it out on your partner, but use bare attention, and the reason for the signal will become clear. It will be a great relief.

Further methods of freeing intuition:

- Recognise the value of intuition (are you convinced now?)
- Face your self-identification with your own ideas.
- Recognise how you reject the ideas of others with the 'not invented here' complex.
- Experience your anxieties and other cues from intuition by applying bare attention.
- Try to recollect times when you had an intuitive recognition of, or made, an intuitive decision. Did the intuitive decision prove to be correct? Recall occasions when you had an 'intuitive signal' and rejected it – what was the outcome?
- Make a written note of intuitive thoughts, particularly if you cannot act on them at the time.

Should intuitive decisions always be accepted? Certainly not! It is a mistake to suppose that intuition is always infallible, coming from some Mystical Source of Absolute Truth, for the world is not so ordered as to be entirely deterministic. Is it then better to apply clear comprehension and deliberate carefully over the intuitive decision when this has been perceived, or simply to take the plunge and go ahead? I cannot answer this – only your intuition will tell you!

Pray tell me, which leg goes after which?

Chapter 7

The Way of Creativeness

Superior work has the quality of an accident. This is not merely a masterful mimicry of the accidental, an assumed spontaneity, in which the careful planning does not show. It lies at a much deeper and genuine level, for what the culture of Taoism and Zen proposes is that one might become the kind of person who, without intending it, is a source of marvellous accidents.

Alan Watts[1]

To arrive at the simplest truth, as Newton knew and practised, requires *years of contemplation*. Not activity. Not reasoning. Not calculating. Not busy behavior of any kind. Not reading. Not talking. Simply *bearing in mind* what it is one needs to know.

G. Spencer-Brown[2]

The difference between an efficient manager and an *effective* one is creativeness. The efficient manager performs the job well, according to rules which have been laid down, or which he or she has worked out. The efficient manager operates from habit. The effective manager also conforms to the rules – but is also aware that while rules and habits are static, reality is dynamic. This manager sees the ever-growing discrepancy between rules and reality, and bears it in mind until – suddenly! – he or she is aware of new possibilities which can transform the situation.

Creativeness is something we do not find discussed or even mentioned in Zen literature, for it is essentially a western concept. Zen prefers to 'do it' rather than talk about it! Perhaps that is one reason why the Zen artists of Japan are among the most creative in the world. The concept itself is very much an abstraction – and Zen does not deal in abstractions, but rather in realities. Let us ask ourselves what these realities are. It is not difficult to discover them from the two quotations above: creativeness is *intuition guided by will.* We have already discussed intuition, but what is the will that guides it? Emphatically not Nietzsche's 'Will to power', not the forcing through of a solution to a problem, but rather *commitment*, the same type of commitment with which it is possible to do the 'work' of Zen. It is the attitude of Cook Ting, of *wu-wei*, watchful composure and always *bearing the problem in mind.*

To make this even clearer, let us say that what we are talking about is not so much *creativity* as the *quality of creativeness*, or in Alan Watts' words, 'being the kind of person who, without intending it, is a source of marvellous accidents'. The experience of such an 'accident' was described by the composer Tchaikovsky:

> Generally speaking, the germ of a future composition comes suddenly and unexpectedly . . . it takes root with extraordinary force and rapidity, shoots up through the earth, puts forth branches and leaves, and finally blossoms. *I cannot define the creative process in any way but by this simile.*[3] (My italics)

Here we come to a vital point: all so-called explanations of the creative process are merely similes, and not for the first time in this book the error of mistaking the map for the territory, the simile or meaphor for the reality, must be pointed out, for the laws governing maps and similes are not those of reality. Please excuse the following absurdity, which springs from a Chinese Taoist source:

Question: Can you stand seven elephants on top of one another? No, but you can write 'elephant' on seven pieces of paper and make a pile of them.

More of the same, but different

As already mentioned, we in the west think of creativity rather than creativeness – we immediately seek results rather than seeking to be the kind of people who achieve them, which is putting the cart before the horse. We look for something which can be measured and therefore controlled (and we frequently reject the 'imponderables'). Creativity is just such a measurable quantity, whereas creativeness is not. It is a quality of the person. Nevertheless, countless western writers, philosophers and scientists have tried to define creativity and find a mechanism for it. Søren Kierkegaard thought that human creativity manifested itself via abrupt and discontinuous transitions that he called qualitative leaps. And so ever since Niels Bohr proposed that light was emitted when an electron made an abrupt and discontinuous quantum jump from one orbit to another, there have been various attempts by neurophysiologists to explain creativity in terms of quantum theory. This is rather like saying that kangaroos behave like electrons, because they too run by making quantum leaps. The psychologist Rollo May defined creativity as 'the process of bringing something new into being'[4] but unfortunately, in this age of 'new and improved' versions of old products, one must then define what is truly 'new'. And, coming back for a moment to Kierkegaard, note that he talked about *qualitative* leaps, whereas the physicists deal with *quantitative* jumps. A very important distinction! Creativeness is a matter of *quality*.

The results of making this mistake – it is one of 'logical typing', as we saw earlier – are to divert creativity into *productivity*; quantity is mistaken for quality. Many examples of this type of error have occurred over the last two decades, when metaphors (in the sense of working hypotheses) for creative behaviour have been distinctly cognitive in orientation, that is to say, creativity is regarded as a particular mode of thinking. Edward de Bono, for example, in his book of the same title has described 'lateral thinking', in which the subject is trained to gain access to memories not usually associated with a particular event.[5] Taking this further, Fisher Idea Systems of Honolulu developed a computerised system of word associations to aid in the process.[6] To evaluate this, an experiment was carried out in which two groups were asked to perform a task, one group with and one without the association lists. The task given was as follows:

> They were seated in a room, given pencil and paper, and shown a T-shirt with a cute drawing of nine ducks playing in a hot tub. They were told: We're going to role-play a situation. You are the idea person for a company that manufactures this kind of product. The artist who works for the company has come up with this design to be printed on T-shirts. Your job is to think of cute or catchy phrases to print under the picture. The point is to think of some saying that will help sell T-shirts, and you need to do this right away. A lot of creative people and some psychologists have all said that the best way to think of good ideas is to have a lot of ideas, without thinking about whether they are good or not . . . Later, you can always go back and pick out the best ones. Right now, just try to think of a lot of ideas.[7]

The result of the experiment was that those who worked with the Fisher list produced significantly more ideas than those who did not. But of the *quality* of the ideas we are told nothing, nor do we have any results to show whether they were truly creative. (What might those be, anyway?) The present author has no experience in selling T-shirts, and cannot evaluate the possible sales success of this method of producing cute phrases for them, but certainly it may have been a good method for Fisher Idea Systems to market *their* product . . .

Systems of this kind, in whatever guise, with whatever 'scientific' justification, can only produce 'more of the same', as can be seen in nearly all the products offered to our consumer society, from TV programmes to cars – and, yes, to T-shirts. All this has *nothing whatever to do with creativeness.*

The mythology of the divided brain

Since the 1960s neurophysiologists, psychologists and many others have tried to reconcile the roles of intuition and imagination in the process of creation with the metaphor that creative thinking is right brain cognition; the left hemisphere of the brain is said to process information logically and linearly, while the right brain processes it simultaneously and 'holistically'. Not all researchers agree, however; R. S. McGallum and S. M. Glynn, for example, wrote in 1979 that, 'the right hemisphere is no doubt involved in the production of creative behaviour. However, at this point in time a conclusion that this hemisphere is the seat of creativity is premature and founded on limited empirical evidence.'[8] Further, the 'right-brain, left-brain' theory of creativity overlooks an important part of the brain, namely the prefrontal lobe, the 'cells of will', and various authors have suggested that these, too, are engaged in creativity. In fact, as we have seen, these are clearly important, being the seat of the will.

But now let us ask the question, can *any metaphor whatever* (in the sense of a working hypothesis) describe the functioning of the brain? The fact is, *no conceivable theory can ever explain it because we have no concept whatever which can provide a satisfactory link between 'brainware' and 'mindware'.* Many have tried to find one, and some, if not all, of the possibilities are given in the endnote.[9]

Another metaphor for creative behaviour is that of the humanistic psychologists such as Carl Rogers and Abraham Maslow, for whom creative people are emotionally healthy and have a fine sense of self. But this is contradicted by others who suggest that one must be slightly neurotic to create. Thus F. Barron wrote, 'the creative person is both more primitive and more cultured, more destructive and more constructive, crazier and saner, than the average person'.[10] Not much help here!

What does this mean to the manager?

You have a right to ask what all this means to you, a practising manager? 'Surely I do not need all this physiology, psychology and philosophy?' Indeed, you do not, and this is precisely the point. For the moment you begin to think about how your mind works and then try to manipulate it by using any theory-inspired methods such as 'right-brain thinking', you will suffer the fate of the centipede:

> The centipede was happy, quite,
> Until a toad in fun
> Said, 'Pray, which leg goes after which?'
> He lay distracted in a ditch,
> Wondering how to run.[11]

All theories of the origin of creativity are obstacles to the creative process, for they beg the question. If it is a creative act to produce a theory about creativity, *how does this happen?* Above all, they have nothing to say about creativeness. Even if you accept such theories or methods *without thinking about them,* just trying to use them because they are in fashion or are dressed up in scientific clothing, you will inevitably manipulate your mind into a state of non-creativeness. And this is what Zen has to tell us.

If one were to try to measure creativity by quantifying what is created, by the number of pieces of music, poems, paintings or even T-shirt slogans produced, this would be to relegate nearly everything that management does to the realm of the purely mechanical. Peter Drucker writes:

> Management is not just passive, adaptive behaviour, but means taking action to make the most desired results come to pass.
>
> Management implies responsibility for attempting to shape the economic environment.
>
> Anybody whose responsibility it is to act – rather than just to know – operates in the future.
>
> There is no 'scientific' way to set objectives for an organisation. They are rightly value judgements . . . one reason for this is that the decisions stand under incurable uncertainty. They are concerned with the future. And we have no 'facts' concerning the future.[12]

Eastern mind, western mind?

Zen and Taoism take a somewhat different view of the mind from that of the west. That is *not* to say that the 'eastern' mind is different from the 'western', as is so often said, for the fact that two people, for instance a gardener and a biologist, take a different view of a rose, does not mean that there are two different roses! (Remember Chapter 3 – 'Do you know how to look at a flower?') Zen, then, considers the mind to be made up, so to speak, of several layers. The first layer is our normal consciousness, in which we generally move. It is dualistically constructed, that is, it sees everything in terms of opposites – black and white, this and that, and it classifies everything with which it comes into contact in accordance with its own preconceived categories. The gardener and the biologist each use their own sets of categories – and as I am sure you have experienced, so do production, marketing and finance managers . . . The conscious mind seeks for polarities, and finds them wherever it looks. Particularly relevant here is that various activities will be classified into 'creative' and non-creative', so that many ideas, perhaps of great potential value, are *rejected almost before they are born.*

The next layer 'down' is the semi-conscious, and here are stored memories which can be brought into full consciousness when they are needed, and which include, as we saw in Chapter 5, associations of an emotive character linked with the memories of objects. Below this again is the 'unconscious', as psychologists normally term it, and here are deeply stored memories and patterns of behaviour, thought and feelings to which we do not normally have conscious access – they function and influence us, but we are not generally aware of them.

This is as far as we in the west normally go in our exploration of the mind, but it is not enough for the understanding of creativeness. We need something more, even if it proves to be something whose existence we cannot demonstrate experimentally.

Question: Why is it impossible to demonstrate the existence of the 'something more'? Is it because experimentation takes place only at the conscious level, and so cannot penetrate deeper? Surely it is because the intellect raises questions about the 'something more', about creativeness, but it cannot answer them.

The bedrock layer of the mind has been given many names, none of which I propose to mention, for that would be to give it some kind of classification in your mind, even if not in mine (I have lived with this problem for years!). But we can refer to it as the 'storehouse of possibilities'. I do not like to give models of such things as this, but so long as you (and I!) remember the words of Chuang Tzu – 'Once you have the meaning you can forget the words . . .' – a model might be useful. And this is a die, for which all possibilities of the numbers which come up exist before it is thrown.[13] And so when Peter Drucker says that there are no facts concerning the future, he is perfectly correct. There are no facts concerning what will come up next time the die is thrown, but the possibilities exist.

But now, please forget the model! For whereas we must throw the die before one of the possibilities can be realised, this is not so with creativeness, for this does not emerge simply from a passive block of wood like a die, but from a living source of possibilities, constantly in motion and forever revealing its secrets. And so it comes to this: It is not 'I' that creates anything: instead, 'I', my conscious self, becomes aware of a new possibility that has always existed. And this is what underlies Peter Drucker's statement that management is not just passive, adaptive behaviour. Managers require creativeness – or they have nothing worthwhile to offer.

The unifying moment

Zen does not reach understanding by studying the minds of other people, constructing hypotheses and theories and then trying to apply them. Instead, understanding is reached through *one's own experience.* Therefore I make no excuse for describing my own experience in writing this book. Here you will notice the similarity to my description of my personal 'signals' of intuition in the last chapter. Intuition and creativeness have much to do with each other.

There have been some times when I did not know where to go next; the word-processor does not help here, however cleverly it records and organises the words which will appear on the printed page. I am conscious of various ideas, and each will have a part to play in the overall scheme. But somehow they do not seem to fit together, the links between the various ideas are missing, and the situation is somewhat confused and also rather dispiriting – perhaps one passage should be left out and something else (which is also already in consciousness) could take its place. But then comes a moment of 'letting go'. I give up trying to impose a pre-conceived structure on my separate ideas, and suddenly feel that all is clear and I can continue, that I know what to do next and that that will, quite without effort, lead me on further. I have not actually recognised a structure on which to work, one I could formulate and write down, but it is there. As Tchaikovsky said, 'it takes root with extraordinary force and rapidity, shoots up through the earth, puts forth branches and leaves, and finally blossoms.' This is the unifying moment, the moment when all the ideas which have been floating idly about take their places. This is not an experience limited to composers or artists or even writers on Zen, but an everyday experience of the ordinary person.

Exercise: Think of occasions when this has happened to you, when, in an apparently confused situation, all has become clear and you could *act*. This need not be limited to your work, it has almost certainly happened in your personal life, too. Now, in preparation for what comes next, think of possible reasons why, in some circumstances, this did not happen, or took a long time. You should be looking at these with bare attention, that is not allowing yourself any valuation of whether what happened was good or bad, right or wrong. In this way you will arive at clear comprehension of yourself.

Creativeness is something entirely natural, like the growth of a tree. And just because it is natural, there is no way in which we can dominate and command it. Instead, what we can do is to remove the obstacles to its growth. And so now we can see the function of the will in creativeness. It is not the will to be creative – creativeness is already present in us, so we have not need to *try to be* creative, and the effort of trying is self-defeating. The will is needed in order to remove the obstacles to the free play of creativity. Let's see what they are.

Letting go the psychic block

Freedom and creativeness are synonymous, and the opposite of freedom is rigidity of the ego. By 'ego' here I do not mean anything metaphysical, but those functions of the mind which can crystallise into a 'psychic block'. And these are what Spencer Brown (quoted at the beginning of this chapter) mentioned: activity, reasoning, calculating, busy behaviour of any kind, reading, talking. Yet creativity is not a matter of 'switching off' all these. They all have to happen, and what is more they must be carried out persistently, with will-power. At the same time there must be the will to bear in mind the problems that surround us – the effective manager is never complacent, never thinks that things are going along in the ideal way, for the simple reason that the ideal never fits the facts, since we do not know them all (and there are none at all about the future). But when all the thinking is done – or before that, for it is a never-ending process, then the unifying moment comes – if we allow it to happen. And this is the 'marvellous accident'.

Creativeness in action

Obviously there are no 'recipes' for creativeness, because any attempt to use a system is itself a psychic block. But we can see some general principles:

- Develop greater awareness of situations and problems, viewing them with bare attention. In this way they will be seen with clarity.
- Look at situations with sincerity. This means recognising and admitting to yourself your own involvement (for example a problem of bad communication has two sides – the other and your own!)
- When you have observed the problem in this way, do not put it on one side, but *bear it mind* for however long is necessary.

- Eventually a solution will occur to you. Take care to notice the intuitive signals, whatever these happen to be in your case.
- Look at the solution you have discovered with *clear comprehension of purpose and suitability.* Not all the intuitive and creative ideas you get are necessarily right or practicable.
- And finally, *act.*

In conclusion

It is only the creative exercise of our individual and collective wills which can make us more humane – and the manager has a great responsibility in just this, in making our society more caring about our fellow inhabitants of this earth and of the earth itself; not merely in making it more efficient.

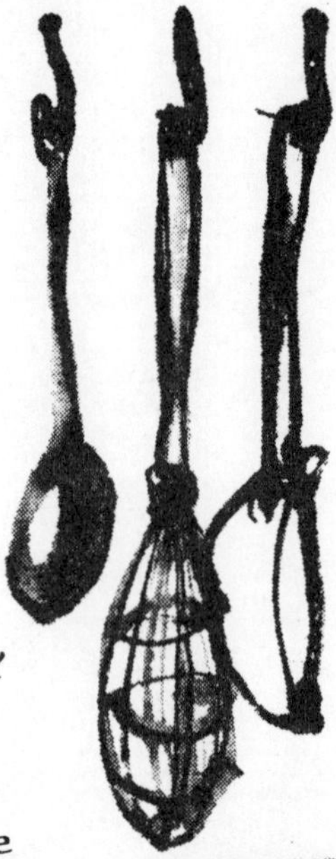

The wheel has thirty spokes with a common hub. It is the hole in the centre which makes it useful.

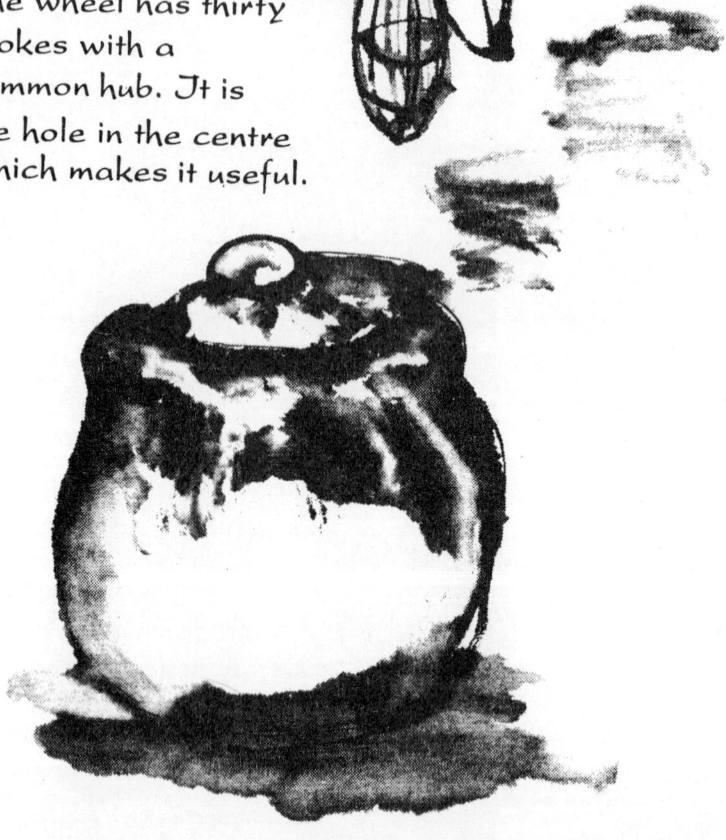

Chapter 8

The Way of the Manager

When you counsel a ruler in the Tao,
Advise him not to use force to conquer
The universe,
For force creates resistance.
Just do what needs to be done.
Never take advantage of power.

Lao Tzu – *Tao Te Ching*[1]

The ancient and famous Chinese classic *Tao Te Ching*, written by Lao Tzu in the sixth century BC, contains a great deal of advice to kings and rulers, and is therefore of great value to managers. It is totally in accord with the spirit of Zen, indeed the word 'Tao' is often to be found in Japanese writings as an equivalent of Zen. What does this word mean? It is an underlying principle out of which all things emerge, and to which they return, but that is not to say that it is an 'original substance' from which everything is made. It is something we can experience in our lives and follow – but because words themselves are 'things', we cannot use them to describe it. But just as we could see Zen in the work of Cook Ting and in the life of

Musashi, so we can discover Tao in our work as managers, always remembering that Tao and Zen are but two expressions of the same principle, quality or spirit – whichever word you like to use.

The Tao of organisations

Every manager lives, works and has his being in an organisation of one sort or another. It gives him opportunities for creative action on the one hand, and on the other it places limitations on his freedom of which he must be constantly aware. But, more than that, in order to be able to take maximum advantage of the opportunities and not be *inwardly frustrated* by the limitations so that they become psychological barriers even to doing what actually *is* possible, he needs a genuine feeling of what an organisation actually *is*.

Naturally, here we are not concerned with the actual structure of organisations and are not discussing the relative merits of strict hierarchies or more flexible forms of management structure. But if we ask how an organisation comes into being, the usual answer we get is that it is something constructed, something put together like a machine out of separate parts. On the surface of things this is true, but to quote an admittedly somewhat abstruse verse from *Tao Te Ching*:

> The great Tao flows everywhere, to left and right.
> The ten thousand things depend on it;
> It holds nothing back.
> It fulfils its purpose silently and makes no claim.

The 'ten thousand things' are everything that exists, including of course what we see as the parts of an organisation, but the 'great Tao' is the principle of growth. It does not call attention to itself, but it is always present. That is, organisations are the product of growth, and like everything that grows – plants for example – they divide themselves into parts, from within outwards, yet remain a whole. When we look at an organisation in this way – or when *you look at your own* – we recognise that even the most highly structured organisation is constantly growing and changing and contains the possibilities for change. The limitations are not as inflexible as they appear on paper, and this is because what is established either in writing or by 'company practice' does not fully describe the organisation, but is only the outward form. Therefore Lao Tzu tells us:

> The wheel has thirty spokes with a common hub;
> It is the hole in the centre which makes it useful.
> The pot is made out of clay;
> It is the space within that makes it useful.
> Take advantage of what is there,
> And also of what is not.

There is always a great deal in an organisation which is never put on paper, and indeed never can be. On the one hand this consists of informal patterns of activity and on the other of the actual personalities involved; these factors, after all, really determine what *actually happens*.

Exercise: Take a look at your organisation in this way. How did it grow? If you are in a large company, this is not so much a matter of reviewing the whole history of the company, but rather of examining that part of it with which you are concerned. This means thinking about the people you deal with as well as the formal relationships. Do this with bare attention, that is without letting your prejudices for or against anyone influence your judgement more than you can help.

Now consider what difficulties and frustrations you experience in your work, and ask yourself whether you have taken both 'what is there' and 'what is not' into account. Be sure to include a thorough examination of your own activities and the *observed* effects of your personality on others. In this way you will come to see new possibilities for yourself. It may well be that the 'problem' which you have formulated does not in reality exist, or, alternatively, can be reformulated in a way which will allow for a creative solution. As a brief example of the latter, I may quote an example out of my own practice:

> T. was an English engineer working in Germany as a marketing manager in a large company and complained that he was very frustrated by the methods of working and the 'company climate' in general, which were far more formal than he was used to. When we examined together in detail exactly what he did in many situations (having changes made to a product, getting his travel documents authorised, etc.) he discovered that in a very real sense he was taking advantage of 'what was not there', and therefore there was no actual problem. (For example, when a customer requested a change in the product he would go to the engineers concerned directly – strictly against the book. Yet he repressed this fact.) But because he had previously thought of the organisation only as it existed on paper, he was in a state of frustration which not only reduced his effectiveness, but brought on severe psychosomatic symptoms.

Communicating naturally

It is a commonplace to say that a manager's work depends on communication, but the principle of 'Just do what needs to be done' – a line from Tao Te Ching which is yet another way of expressing *wu-wei* – is vital here. Let us look at it from both sides, the listener's and the speaker's. But first, please spend a little time thinking about that phrase from Lao Tzu.

Question: What is there which does *not* need to be done? What mental processes do you go through unnecessarily which hinder you in doing what you really want to do? Anxiety? Worry? Thinking about how you are thinking? With what you have learned about yourself in your training sessions, you may find other, quite different but equally unnecessary examples. Now let us apply this to communicating. Here is what Zen Master Shunryu Suzuki (founder of the first Zen Center in America) has to say:

> When you listen to someone you should give up all your preconceived ideas and your subjective opinions; you should just listen to him, just observe what his way is. We put very little emphasis on right or wrong or good and bad. We just see things as they are with him, and accept them. This is how we communicate with each other. Usually when you listen to some statement, you hear it as a kind of echo of yourself. *You are actually listening to your own opinion*. If it agrees with your opinion you may accept it or you may not even hear it. That is one danger when you listen to someone. The other danger is to be caught by the statement. If you do not understand your master's statement in its true sense, you will easily be caught by something which is involved in your own subjective opinion, or by some particular way the statement is expressed. You will take what he says only as a statement, without understanding the spirit between the words. This kind of danger is always there.[2]

Exercise: Has it happened to you while you have been reading this book (and it would be surprising if it had not), that whilst with your eyes you have read what was said, your own opinions have prevented you from understanding it? Naturally I am not suggesting that you should always agree with me, but before you can reach a valid agreement or disagreement, you first have to take in what you read. In the worst case, one's mind is so full of one's own opinions that the eyes merely skim over the words.

Another exercise: Have there been any phrases or statements in the book which have apparently so exactly corresponded to your own opinion that you might have missed their *real* meaning? Could you have been 'caught' by a pleasant turn of phrase or by the fact that you have at some time used the same words, or you read them elsewhere and you agreed with them? This time the meaning *might* be different! And finally, you might reflect on some recent meeting or discussion during which there was a disagreement. Try to recall exactly what happened and analyse the causes of the problem. No doubt, you were only partly to blame – but what was your part?

When we think about how we express ourselves, the natural way is to do so *out of silence*, out of Tao. But, as Suzuki continues:

> To be natural to ourselves, and also to follow what others say or do in the most appropriate way, is quite difficult. If we try to adjust ourselves intentionally in some way, it is impossible to be natural. If you try to adjust yourself in a certain way, you will lose yourself.[3]

If a sales director, for example, tries to project an image of himself which he feels is appropriate to the sales conference he is addressing, he will most likely fail to motivate his audience to further and greater success. For there is a great difference between the way we like to think of ourselves and the way we actually are. And, make no mistake, the sales director's lack of sincerity with himself will be picked up intuitively by his audience. ('You can fool some of the people some of the time, but . . .') This is also true on the scale of the company, for in spite of the most ingenious and thorough attempts by marketing and PR people to project the desired image of the company through the media, insincerity can only be concealed for a time. 'Good advertising, lousy product' is never a way to continued business success.

One of our most frequent objectives in communication is persuasion, and silence has two important roles here. On the one hand, to be persuasive, your whole mind and body must be in action, and you must speak from your inner silence. On the other hand, *you must allow your audience to perceive what you are saying in their own silence.* This means you should not argue with them, but rather listen to their objections until they *see for themselves* that they are not valid. In this way you will be following Lao Tzu's advice not to use force, for 'force creates resistance'. This is 'sales resistance', for you are, after all, trying to 'sell' your ideas – and the customer is always (*to be treated as if he is)* right.

Communication is strategy

We began to look at communication as strategy when we discussed persuasion, but rather than list all the various functions of communication and then work out a strategy for each, I propose to look at the way in which you, the manager, can develop strategies for yourself. Only then can all cases which are important to you be covered completely appositely. We already know the two basic principles needed for this – clear comprehension of purpose and clear comprehension of suitability.

Purpose has many levels. At the deepest of these, in our context, it is the answer to the 'Why am I a manager?' question – it would be surprising if you had finished with that yet. To begin at the uppermost level and take actual examples, ask yourself why you are writing a letter, making a phone call or going to a discussion or meeting. A thousand different reasons are possible on the surface, but what lies beneath them? For instance, what aspects of yourself are you trying to present? A really honest answer to this question will only emerge if you examine it with bare attention. It could be some such as 'to make a good impression on the boss', or out of anxiety about some aspect of your situation. In other words, something *not directly connected with the actual purpose you consciously intend and therefore something which does not need to be done.* Now I am not saying that you should immediately try to put this aside

– it might be important – but simply that you should *recognise and be aware of it*, for only then will you be able to evolve the best possible strategy for your communication, and only then will you function effectively *out of your own nature*.

When it comes to a meeting at which various plans and points of view are being discussed, it is certain that those who are perfectly clear about their own motives are most likely to succeed in their true purpose. Whether you have decided to use Musashi's sword or Cook Ting's knife, whether the occasion requires constructive aggression, psycho-politics or the soft sell is quite irrelevant; the first step towards evolving a successful strategy is to know why you are evolving it.

Practice: To practise clear comprehension of purpose continually is of very great benefit. It is a practice which strengthens such qualities as energy, endurance and concentration. On the other hand it brings to notice *incorrectly perceived motives*. You will become aware that sometimes you do the right thing for the wrong reasons – but that just as often, you do the wrong thing!

As we saw earlier, clear comprehension of suitability is the art of the practicable. What do you intend to achieve in your strategy, and is this achievable, taking into account the nature of those you will be communicating with? Are you actually capable of carrying out the communication? To realise that you are not is halfway to discovering how you can become so. And, finally and most basically, is your strategy really suited to your *actual* purpose? Look at this with bare attention, because you may discover that you have preferences for ways of communicating which are not always ideal for the purpose.

Exercise: I have tried to convey the message to you that communication emerges from silence – and used a lot of words to do it! So the question is, was it successful? Consider what has been said carefully, not only as regards its content, but also its style and method. How would you have improved it?

Meeting stress with elasticity

Who can wait quietly until the mud settles?
Who can remain still until the moment of action?

Lao Tzu

The mind that 'has Zen' is an elastic mind, able to meet every situation in life with equanimity and with all its faculties alert, ready for decisive and effective action. This is the 'reward' that all the hard work involved can bring. Even situations in which there is no hope, in which disaster is unavoidable, can be met in this way, so that new opportunities can be seen or at least ways discovered to rescue what can be rescued. This is the benefit of the elastic mind.

When reading the story of Cook Ting for the first time, you may have had a sense of the natural rhythm of the man as he worked, as I did. He did not rush hectically at the job, neither did he waste time; one feels he was completely relaxed in his activity. But this is not the situation of most managers. Instead, they are stressed by the pressure of too much work, by responsibilities, and very often personal problems make things worse. And therefore a great deal of attention is paid by psychologists, psychotherapists and many others to finding ways to alleviate stress. Our object here is a different one; not to *cure* the results (symptoms) of stress, but to *eliminate or reduce its effects* on us. This is the contribution of Zen.

Let us look at the problem in a somewhat different way. When we speak of 'stress' in this connection, we are actually using the word incorrectly. In the sense in which it is used in engineering science, stress means the load applied, for example, to a piece of metal (strictly speaking, the force per unit cross-section). Under the action of this load, the metal *deforms*, that is it stretches, is compressed or bends, and the amount by which it deforms is called the 'strain'. There is a mathematical relationship between the stress and the strain, which is such that the amount of strain produced by a given load is determined by the *elasticity* of the metal, this being a property of the particular metal. Further than this, there is a *limit of elasticity*. When this is reached, the metal breaks.

The analogy is clear. How much stress of work and responsibility a manager can take before he loses effectiveness, suffers ill health or breaks down completely depends on his elasticity of mind: Zen proposes, therefore, that we should increase this. Here, after all, is the only possible answer, for unless a manager gives up his job completely, there is little that he can do to reduce the stress. True, he can reorganise his work and delegate some of it – but the responsibility remains.

Finding the natural rhythm

Lao Tzu wrote: 'Stillness is the lord of activity.' This could serve as a motto for us. It is the basic principle of all Zen – both in training and action. One sits still for a while and then, as Shunryu Suzuki picturesquely said, 'When I sit on my cushion I am nothing; when I get up I make the whole world.' You have probably noticed this in your training sessions – when they are ended there is a feeling of having been refreshed and a readiness to 'dive headfirst into worldly activity'. Once you have experienced this it can be extended beyond the twenty minutes or so of daily training. For life is not a conveyor belt, moving without pause; even at its most hectic, there are moments of silence.

Exercise: Try to observe this happening in the life around you. For example a good speaker has a rhythm of moving forward with what he is saying, then making a pause. One can often notice a similar rhythm in a meeting or discussion. A successfully constructive one always has its moments of silence, when people are collecting their thoughts; if this does not happen and everyone is talking all the time, the result is chaos! Look for other examples of this. Life is not, however, like driving in heavy traffic when there are continual stops. These are forced on us, whereas the rhythm we are looking for is quite natural, and comes from the deepest parts of our being – yet is not hidden. To find it, first discover actual examples, then *bear the rhythm in mind*, not forcing yourself to take obligatory rests, but letting the rhythm come naturally.

Living with uncertainty

What is uncertainty? It is the knowledge that there are things which we cannot predict and control – and this is a constant source of anxiety, which means stress. There is a tension between what we want and hope and the ever-present, *but often suppressed*, awareness that there is no guarantee that things will turn out that way. This stress can almost literally tear one apart. Zen shows us that our ability for prediction and control – the ability of logic and reason – is limited. Therefore, *there is no other way but to accept this*. Emphatically, however, this is not fatalism, the abandonment of all effort because there is nothing to be done about the situation. The open mind, the mind that sees things clearly, knows that there are limits to its logic and extends them with its intuitive powers – but also knows that even these are ultimately limited in the face of events.

Practice: The only way to understand the nature and effects of uncertainty is to *look at it in yourself.* By this is not meant dwelling on one's anxieties, but observing, with bare attention, whether you yourself are actually predictable in everything you do. Of course you are not – and life would be utterly boring if you were! Here is the key to living with uncertainty – discover it as that which makes life worth living.

Why am I a manager?

This question may not have been in the forefront of your mind, yet quite probably has persisted as you have been reading this book. What kind of a question is it? It is not the same as asking of a company, 'Why are we in business', for we have known the answer to that for a long time – it is, as Henry Ford first said, to provide a service, it being a 'law of business' that this was its object rather than profit.[4] For Ford's laws of business, Peter Drucker substituted 'the objective needs of the enterprise' and also spoke of 'objective laws', which he distinguished strictly from the 'personal preferences' of the manager.[5]

Is it ultimately satisfying for the manager to act in accordance with such laws? To try to do so is a great cause of stress and strain, for, as Zen tells us, *the laws are illusory;* no laws which we can formulate can take all the facts into account. Yet if we believe that there are such laws, the conviction that we can control the world inevitably follows. Zen sees through this delusion, and the planet on which we live is telling us in no uncertain manner just what kind of delusion it is, and what it effects are. (As you may know, the Zen culture of Japan is imbued with a deep love of nature, and the delusion which leads to its destruction is seen through. But this is a subject for another occasion.)

The effect of this delusion on the manager himself is to cause him to try to mould himself according to an image of what he supposes will best serve the 'objective laws of the business'. The conflict between this and his personal preferences is the origin of the frustrated sense of 'not knowing where all this is leading' and, in the extreme case, 'executive burn-out.'

The answer to this is not a revolution against all rules and conventions, for it is notorious that violent revolutions create worse tyrannies than those they destroy. It is instead to recognise and bring to a peaceful end the conflict between what we think we are and what we actually are, to ensure that we allow ourselves space for the 'personal preferences', and so express the flowing nature of our own being. And this is to become truly human – acting thinking and speaking according to what we actually are.

The fish-trap exists because of the fish. Once you've caught the fish you can forget the trap.

Chapter 9

The Way Ahead

The fish-trap exists because of the fish.
Once you've caught the fish, you can forget the trap.
Words exist because of their meaning;
Once you've caught the meaning, you can forget the words.
Where can I find a man who has forgotten words,
So that I can have a word with him?

Chuang Tzu[1]

The way ahead goes far beyongd the confines of this book, which is, after all, not an encyclopaedia of knowledge about management nor a directory of techniques, but simply a sign-post to effectiveness. This, to return once more to Peter Drucker, is crucial to a person's development, raising not only his or her own performance level, but also that of the whole organisation. And development is a process which never ends. This is clear from Zen training, as it has been carried out in the temples of Japan for more than a thousand years, and in China before that. At some stage a monk may reach 'satori', that is, an experience of clarity and freedom, but this is never final, and so he continues in his practice. So also must the manager, for whatever he or she achieves will only be a step on the way. Nevertheless, the Chinese say that 'a journey of a thousand miles begins with a single step'. And that is how I would like you to regard this book, as simply a beginning.

It might be asked why more specific examples of situations in which managers find themselves and in which Zen can help them have not been given, or why the exercises for practice do not relate directly to the activities of management. Firstly, in no way is Zen specific to managers, any more than it is, say, to archery, tea-drinking or any other art or activity of living. Instead *it is specific to human beings.* Secondly, no two people are alike, nor do they develop in the same ways, or even by exactly the same processes, so that any attempt to produce a standardised procedure for the development of effectiveness is bound to end in failure for most. Here one might compare the situation with military training, which is a completely standardised set of methods for training *efficient* soldiers. But we said at an early stage that there is a world of difference between efficiency and effectiveness, and the difference is Zen – clarity, sincerity, intuition and creativeness within an open mind.

Yet managers, like soldiers, need techniques, otherwise they could not do their work. The difference is that the soldier who throws his weapon away is heading for serious trouble, whereas problems lie ahead for a manager if he does *not* discard his techniques when they have either served their purpose or no longer meet existing (and ever-changing) conditions – whether this is because managers fail to recognise what is happening or because they identify personally with the way they have always done their jobs or with the organisations they have built up. In other words, management techniques are 'throw-away' tools, like Chuang Tzu's fish-trap.

But of course this is a very limited view of Zen! For Zen is a Way of Wisdom, and wisdom is not in itself knowledge, but *the best application of knowledge,* as the Grand Tea Master Soshitsu Sen tells us in the quotation at the beginning of this book. Above all, Zen concerns itself with the whole human being, whatever he or she does, at every moment of his life. And in this it is quite unlike Old Benjamin, the cynical donkey in George Orwell's *Animal Farm*, for whom hunger, hardship and disappointment were the unalterable conditions of life, and 'life will go on as it always has done – that is, badly.' For the Way of Zen is the way to openness and opportunity. Take this Way, as Musashi said, 'with a trustworthy heart. You must train diligently.'[2]

Further reading and Notes

Introduction The Way is as Clear as Daylight

1. Daisetz T. Suzuki, in Introduction to *Zen in the Art of Archery*, trans. Eugen Herrigel, New York: Random House, 1989.
2. The noted Zen writer Alan Watts said this: 'If Zen is regarded as having the same function as a religion in the west, we shall naturally want to find some logical connection between its central experience (*satori*) and the improvement of human relations. But this is actually putting the cart before the horse. The point is that some such experience or way of life as this is the object of improved human relations'. (Alan W. Watts, *The Way of Zen*, London: Penguin, 1990.)
3. Miyamoto Musashi, *A Book of Five Rings*, trans. Victor Harris, London: Allison & Busby, 1987.

PART 1 – ZEN IS . . .

Chapter 1 The Way of Effectiveness

1. Peter F. Drucker, *The Effective Executive*, New York: HarperCollins, 1985.

2. *The Zen Teaching of Rinzai*, trans. Irmgard Schloegl, Shambhala, 1976.
3. Peter Drucker spent considerable time in Japan, and most of his books were translated into Japanese. In 1966 he was awarded the Third Order of Merit by the Japanese government in recognition of his contribution to the development of management in Japan.
4. Chuang Tzu, *Basic Writings*, trans. Burton Watson, New York: Columbia University Press, 1964. *Also*, Kuang-Ming Wu, *The Butterfly as Companion*, New York: State University of New York Press.

Chapter 2 The Way of Clarity

1. *Bankei Zen*, trans. Peter Haskel, New York: Grove-Weidenfeld, 1988.
2. Daisetz T. Suzuki, *Zen and Japanese Culture*, Princeton: Princeton University Press, 1959.

Chapter 3 The Way of Action

1. Miyamoto Musashi, *A Book of Five Rings*, trans. Victor Harris, London: Allison and Busby, 1987.
2. ibid.
3. ibid.
4. *Bankei Zen*, trans. Peter Haskel, New York: Grove-Weidenfeld, 1988.
5. The following comment is intended for those who have some acquaintance with Zen and may find this contrary to their ideas:

   It is certainly true that some schools of Zen do practise 'Za-Zen', that is sitting in meditation, almost exclusively. But the great Master Bankei, who lived in the 17th century, said in one of his sermons: 'As for Za-Zen, since *za* is the Buddha Mind's sitting at ease, while *zen* is another name for Buddha mind, the Buddha mind's sitting at ease is what is meant by *za-zen*. So when you are abiding in the Unborn, *all the time is za-zen; meditation isn't just the time when you're practising formal meditation* . . . You can't very well do nothing but sleep, so you get up, and you can't just keep on talking, so I let you practise meditation. But this has nothing to do with *rules*! (*Bankei Zen*, op. cit.)

6. The term 'Void' is an important one in Buddhist philosophy and means something like 'meaning which has no meaning'. Therefore *wu-wei* corresponds to it, for this term means 'action and non-action'. This can, however, only be realised in practice – it cannot be grasped intellectually.
7. Daisetz T. Suzuki, *Zen and Japanese Culture*, Princeton, Princeton University Press, 1959.
8. ibid.

Chapter 4 The Way of Sincerity

1. *Mumonkan*, a 13th century Japanese monk.
2. *Hamlet*, I, iii.
3. Sir George Samsom, *Japan, a Short Cultural History*, London: Cresset Library, 1987.
4. Daisetz T. Suzuki, *Zen and Japanese Culture*, Princeton: Princeton University Press, 1959.
5. ibid.

PART 2 – OPENING THE MIND

Chapter 5 The Way of Mindfulness

1. The subject-matter of this chapter does not come from Japanese or Chinese sources, but from an early Buddhist scripture, the 'Satipatthana Sutta'. This is a manual of training in mindfulness, originating in sermons preached by

the Buddha. It is the essential foundation of all later teachings, and is the basis of meditation in all Zen schools. For a detailed exposition of the Sutta, the reader is referred to: Nyaponika Thera, *The Heart of Buddhist Meditation*, London: Rider.
2. Nyaponika Thera, op. cit.

Chapter 6 The Way of Intuition

1. Miyamoto Musashi, *A Book of Five Rings*, trans. Victor Harris, London: Allison and Busby, 1987.
2. To avoid any possible confusion, we are not concerned with instincts here, though these are frequently mistaken for intuition. Instincts are the basic urges directed towards survival, which we have in common with animals. Intuition is an altogether higher function, which we may suppose animals have not developed.
3. 'Hiring media executives is 60% cerebral, 40% visceral', *Media Decisions*, 14, p. 132, 1979.
4. Peter Drucker (op. cit.) says: 'The five elements of decision-making are classical and thoroughly correct. These are:

   1. Is this a generic situation or an exception?
   2. What are the objective conditions the decision has to reach, i.e. 'boundary conditions'?
   3. The thinking through what is 'right' . . . before attention is given to compromises, adaptations and concessions needed to make the decision acceptable.
   4. The building into the decision of the action needed to carry it out.
   5. The 'feedback' which tests the validity and effectiveness of the decision against the actual course of events.

   However, the world might never have enjoyed the blessing of the Big Mac if these principles had been followed by Ray Kroc.

5. In the 1950s the Ford Motor Company carried out the most extensive market and motivation research which had ever been made, to determine the design of a new car, which was named 'Edsel' after one of Henry Ford's sons. It proved to be the greatest failure in automobile history, and cost the company several hundred million dollars. The reason for this seemed to be that the car was in every respect so 'average' that nobody wanted to have it – it had no individuality, which is a quality which car buyers very much want. Intuition, had it been allowed to function rather than be swamped by the volume of market research, might have revealed this, for if the managers concerned had allowed themselves to think for a moment of their own *personal* experience in buying cars, they would probably have realised their mistake.

Chapter 7 The Way of Creativeness

1. Alan W. Watts, *The Way of Zen*, London: Penguin, 1990.
2. G. Spencer-Brown, *Laws of Form*, New York: Dutton, 1979.
3. Willis Harman and Howard Rheingold, *Higher Creativity*, J.P. Tarcher, 1984.
4. Rollo May, *The Courage to Create*, New York: Bantam Doubleday Dell, 1984.
5. Edward de Bono, *Lateral Thinking: a textbook of creativity*, London: Penguin, 1990.
6. Marshall Fisher, *Word Association Lists*, Honolulu.
7. David L. Watson, 'Enhancing creative productivity with the Fisher Association Lists', *The Journal of Creative Behavior*, 23, 1989.
8. 'Hemispheric specialization and creative behavior', R.S. McGallum and S.M. Glynn, *The Journal of Creative Behavior*, 13, 1979.
9. In order to show just how little we know about this, I give here a list of some of the ideas about the mind-body problem which the philosophers have offered us through the ages. The reader may take his choice.

Descartes: interactionism; two separate, and interacting processes.
Spinoza: parallelism; two separate, independent, but perfectly correlated processes.
Malebranche: occasionalism; two separate and independent processes, correlated by God.
Democritus: materialism; a single underlying physical reality.
Subjective idealism, Berkeley: a single underlying mental or spiritual reality.
Hume: phenomenalism; there are neither minds nor bodies, but only ideas resulting from sense impressions.
Russell: double-aspect view; two processes asssumed to be a function of underlying unity.
Hobbes: Epiphenomalism; mind assumed to be a non-causal by-product of body.

10. F. Barron, 'The psychology of imagination', *Scientific American*, 199, 3, 1958.
11. Alan W. Watts, *The Way of Zen*, London: Penguin, 1990.
12. Peter F. Drucker, *The Practice of Management*, Oxford: Heinemann Professional, 1989.
13. It is just here that there is an analogy with quantum physics, (an *analogy*, not a description). 'The development of the Schrdinger wave equation generates an endlessly proliferating number of possibilities . . . *of different branches of reality*!' See: Gary Zukav, *The Dancing Wu Li Masters: overview of the new physics*, London: Fontana, 1984.

Chapter 8 The Way of the Manager

1. There are many translations of *Tao Te Ching*, but none is actually cited here, as the quotations are combined from several versions. For its reading pleasure and superb photographs I recommend *Tao Te Ching*, trans. Gia-Fu Feng and Jane English, Vintage Books.

2. Shunryu Suzuki, *Zen Mind, Beginner's Mind,* USA, Weatherhill.
3. ibid.
4. Henry Ford and Samuel Crowther, *My Life and Work,* reprint of 1922 ed. New York: Ayer.
5. Peter F. Drucker, *The Practice of Management*, Oxford: Heinemann Professional, 1989.

Chapter 9 The Way Ahead

1. Chuang Tzu, *Basic Writings,* trans. Burton Watson, New York: Columbia University Press, 1964.
2. Miyamoto Musashi, *A Book of Five Rings*, trans. Victor Harris, London: Allison and Busby, 1987.